THE RETURN OF PYTHEAS

ALSO BY PASCHALIS NIKOLAOU

As Editor

12 Greek Poems After Cavafy

As Co-editor

Translating Selves : Experience and Identity Between Languages and Literatures
The Perfect Order : Selected Poems 1974-2010 of Nasos Vayenas
Richard Berengarten : A Portrait in Inter-Views

Paschalis Nikolaou

The Return of Pytheas

Scenes from British and Greek Poetry in Dialogue

Shearsman Books

First published in the United Kingdom in 2017 by
Shearsman Books
50 Westons Hill Drive
Emersons Green
BRISTOL
BS16 7DF

www.shearsman.com

ISBN 978-1-84861-567-0

Copyright © Paschalis Nikolaou, 2017

The right of Paschalis Nikolaou to be identified as the author of this work has been asserted by him in accordance with the Copyrights, Designs and Patents Act of 1988.
All rights reserved.

Contents

Acknowledgments   7

Prologue: Poets, Editors, and Seafarers   9

One
'The *Iliad* Suits You': Christopher Logue's Homer – from *Patrocleia* (1962) to the Posthumous Edition of *War Music* (2015)

1. The Troy That Modernism Built   17
2. Paint it Red: Between Logue's
    Early Experiences and an 'Account'   26
3. Intertextuality, Anachronisms, Re-animations   30
4. Drafts and Fragments   36

Two
Translating as Part of the Poetry

1. Before and After Ted Hughes   41
2. Fragment as Method: On Josephine Balmer   49
3. Back to the Start: Alice Oswald
    and an 'Excavation' of the *Iliad*   62

Three
The Travelling Players

1. 'Poems for Friends in Greece 1967-1971':
    Richard Berengarten's Greek Experience   71
2. In Memory of George Seferis / After T. S. Eliot   76
3. Anthologies of Presence   90
4. Collections of In-betweenness   100

Four
The Shade of Cavafy

1. Early Encounters   112
2. Contemporary Stances   116

Afterword: Periplous   130

Bibliography   136
Index   148

Acknowledgments

Parts of this book have their beginnings in doctoral research conducted at the University of East Anglia between 2001 and 2006; my supervisors there, Clive Scott and Jean Boase-Beier (now Professors Emeritus and Emerita) provided valued advice throughout my years in Norwich. Some of my arguments have developed over time, or I took the opportunity to update them as this book was being prepared. I first discussed Christopher Logue's *War Music* in a 2003 review for the *London Magazine*, then helmed by Sebastian Barker. Following a conference at the University of Salford in 2004, an essay appeared in *Translating and Interpreting Conflict* (Rodopi, 2007; edited by Myriam Salama-Carr). Considerations of Josephine Balmer's work were included in the Proceedings of the 5th International Portsmouth Translation Conference (2005; edited by Ian Kemble and Carol O'Sullivan) as well as in vol. 16 of *Norwich Papers* (2008). A 2006 review of Richard Berengarten's *Black Light* for *Modern Poetry in Translation* as well as my contribution to the *Critical Companion* (2011/2016) on his poetry feature components further explored here. Arguments on classical translation and versions by Simon Armitage and Alice Oswald were broached in a review essay for *The AALITRA Review* (no. 9; 2014), while the Summer 2004 issue of *In Other Words* hosted early thoughts on Christopher Reid. Some presences of Cavafy in British poetry were first presented in a conference on translating the literature of small European languages at the University of Bristol (September 2014) and continued to be explored at the inaugural Cavafy Summer School (Athens, July 2017), hosted by the Onassis Foundation and The Cavafy Archive.

Panayotis Kelandrias, Yorgos Kentrotis, Sotirios Keramidas, and Anastasia Parianou have been especially encouraging among my colleagues at the Ionian University's Department of Foreign Languages, Translation and Interpreting, where I have taught since 2007; Aishwarya Subramanyam has carefully perused most sections in this study; David Ricks provided some valuable notes on Cavafy's reception in Britain; and Richard Pine, of The Durrell Library of Corfu, pointed me to varied appearances of Cavafy within Lawrence Durrell's work.

Many poetry extracts, critical texts and translations appear in this book and I am grateful to the following publishers and copyright holders for their help with respect to permissions: Agenda Editions, for 'Snow' by Josephine Balmer, from *Letting Go*; Bloodaxe Books for ''78 Nights' and 'Philomela' by Josephine Balmer, from *Chasing Catullus: Poems, Translations & Transgressions*; Carcanet Press for 'Fever of Kleitos', included in John Ash's *In the Wake of the Day*; the University of Chicago Press for a quotation from Richmond Lattimore's translation of the *Iliad*; Eland Publishing and John Lucas for his poem, 'The Cemetery at Molivos'; Hilary Davies and the Estate of Sebastian Barker for excerpts from *The Land of Gold*, published by Enitharmon Press; Faber and Faber for 'The Cochineal' by Christopher Reid, from *The Curiosities*, as well as for excerpts from the following: Gavin Ewart's *Selected Poems*; Christopher Logue's *War Music, Selected Poems* and autobiography, *Prince Charming*; Alice Oswald's *Memorial*; and Simon Armitage's Introductions to his versions of *The Odyssey* and *The Iliad*, as well as material quoted from *Selected Translations* of Ted Hughes, edited by Daniel Weissbort. Thanks are also due to Farrar, Straus and Giroux for permission to reprint passages from Logue's *War Music*, and also to W. W. Norton for extracts from Simon Armitage and Alice Oswald; Jonathan Cape for permission to reprint the opening of 'Tithonus', from *Falling Awake* by Alice Oswald, published by Jonathan Cape; reproduced by permission of The Random House Group Ltd. ©2016; Penguin Random House for permission to quote excerpts from *The Iliad* by Homer, translated by Robert Fagles. Translation copyright © 1990 by Robert Fagles. Used by permission of Viking Books, an imprint of Penguin Publishing Group, a division of Penguin Random House LLC. All rights reserved; *Poetry* and David Ricks for his poem, 'Cavafy's Stationery'; Salt Publishing for lines from Josephine Balmer's *The Word for Sorrow*, and Vesna Goldsworthy's *Angel of Salonika*; and Shearsman Books for 'Erotic Tales' and 'Sarpedon's Version' from Balmer's *The Paths of Survival*, and for several excerpts from the works of Richard Berengarten, Kelvin Corcoran, Peter Riley and Alice Kavounas. Finally, warm thanks to Tony Frazer for his invaluable support in the final stages of assembling this book.

Many of the poets discussed in this study have provided feedback and assistance at various junctures of my research into their work. Their advice has extended far beyond giving permissions. I feel fortunate for the many conversations that have taken place over the years – as well as for those that will surely follow.

Prologue

Poets, Editors, and Seafarers

This study surveys aspects of dialogue between two literary traditions. Most of the poets whose work is explored here have worked between 1960 and 2017, and most of the poems or translations discussed have also been published in this period. However, *The Return of Pytheas* inevitably assumes a much lengthier history of access to texts, going all the way back to the *Iliad*. For the classical past inevitably shadows the present: George Steiner has observed the frequency with which Achilles and Odysseus are addressed by English-speaking poets. Indeed, he explicitly echoes these poets when he affirms that it is '[…] to the "topless towers of Ilium" and the shores of Ithaka, it is to "deep-browed Homer" that English-language sensibility turns and returns, incessantly, as if striving to appropriate to itself, to the native genius, material already, by some destined or elective affinity, its own' (1996: 91). Working more than a century ago, the first Anglophone modernists further intensified a classical imperative in the poetic mind, especially in their use of themes and through their settings and re-settings of translations.

Moreover, among Anglophone writers, there has been a sustained imaginative desire for the two cultures to connect and to validate each other. In *The Extraordinary Voyage of Pytheas the Greek: The Man Who Discovered Britain* (2001), Barry Cunliffe tells us how, around 330 BC, this adventurer set out from the colony of Massalia (contemporary Marseille) to explore the 'fabled, terrifying lands of Northern Europe', landing on British shores three centuries earlier than Julius Caesar, and then moving on to the Baltic regions and to 'Ultima Thule', that is, Iceland. Historical record is certainly more cognizant of the parts played by Roman (and later Anglo-Saxon and Scandinavian) incursions and colonisations than of any Greek visitors in Britain's linguistic, cultural and civic heritage. But here, as with similar tales – those about possible discoveries of the American continent far earlier than the voyage of Columbus, for instance – there is a sense of a parallel storyline, one that may serve not only to thicken a sense of heritage and deepen a national consciousness, but also to explain, or at least, contextualise a number of identifications. References to Pytheas and his lost account, entitled *On the Ocean*, are to be found in Polybius, Pliny the Elder and the geographer Dicaearchus, among others.

As a historical personage, this intrepid Greek mariner is therefore both curious and mysterious enough in outline to fire up creative thought, not unlike an Egyptian statue inexplicably discovered, say, somewhere in India. One such example is the poetry chapbook by Lesley Saunders, published fifteen years after Cunliffe's volume and discussed at the end of this study. In the intervening chapters, the figure of the ancient Greek seafarer comes to symbolise a rich panoply of encounters: of a poet with another land and people; of expressions and resolutions in verse of the experiences of travel, long stays abroad, and relocation. We veer from case studies to thematic approaches in cataloguing some recent literary 'moments' and to exploring particular modes of exchange between poets and literary traditions. Even so, *The Return of Pytheas* claims to offer no more than a series of additions to an already voluminous list: in its attempts to understand relationships between Greek and British poetry, it is a discussion, indeed, of particular 'scenes', rather than an attempt at a comprehensive or exhaustive account. These are also ongoing dialogues; and new names and interactions are constantly being added.

In linguistic terms, there has long been a trading of places. In antiquity, alongside Latin, the status of the Greek language was comparable to that of English today: a necessary stage in a civilised education and a common code in mediating between other nations and languages. While this present volume begins with the publication of Christopher Logue's *Patrocleia* in 1962, even the briefest consideration of Greek echoes reminds us of the sheer weight of classical poetry and drama as progenitors of world literature. Productions of the past – written in Greek, English, and in other languages – heavily, and, it seems, inescapably permeate modern poetry. A simple mention of forms like the eclogue or the epigram, the significance of Milton's 'Lycidas' (1637), of Keats's 'Ode on a Grecian Urn' (1819), and even the presence of the invented, Cavafy-sounding Phlebas the Phoenician in part IV of *The Waste Land* (1922; see also chapter 3: p. 86 in this book) allow us to intimate durations as well as the range of responses involved. Robert Hass's Introduction to *The Greek Poets: Homer to the Present* (2010) – perhaps the most encompassing account yet of Greek verse through the ages – includes several such realisations: of an entirely fruitful association of poetic traditions, and of literary movements that insistently experiment on and rework what has come before. Among other things, Hass reminds us how, for the early Anglophone modernists, Greek poetry presented a return to 'powerful origins':

> As if to press the point, Pound's *Cantos* begin, notoriously, with an English translation – a translation into almost Anglo-Saxon English – of a Latin translation of a bit from *The Odyssey*, as if to say that there is no setting out without Homer, no setting out without the revisioning in the act of translation. (2010: xxx)

Modern Greek literature is itself intricately linked to the words, modes and thematic inheritance of this past, as is clearly suggested in the very titles of key studies, such as David Ricks's *The Shade of Homer: A Study in Modern Greek Poetry* (1989) and Karen Van Dyck's *Kassandra and the Censors: Greek Poetry Since 1967* (1998). Highlighting this direct inheritance of course also serves to facilitate a quickened understanding of the contacts and connections that recent Greek poetry shares with other literatures. At the same time, such linking can itself lead equally to *mis*understandings, to easy assumptions which may inhibit depiction of the complex, contemporary experience of a nation, as its creative voices process it and relate it. It is perhaps suitable, then, to further track this situation by references to some recent anthologies – and their paratexts – as they attempt to introduce and contextualise Greek poets for an English-speaking readership. David Connolly describes particular challenges thus, in his Preface to a bilingual edition of a collection by Yannis Kondos:

> Translators of modern Greek poets are perhaps further disadvantaged in their efforts to communicate their tradition in the English-speaking world. *The very fact of being obliged to refer to 'modern' Greek poets and not simply Greek poets is indicative of the problem. Experience has taught me that any reference to 'Greek' alone is invariably identified in the mind of the audience or readership with Greek antiquity. Many contemporary poets who have failed to make any impact in English translation have undoubtedly suffered from the legacy of Greece's ancient past and from a particular perception of Greece by Westerners.* The absence in their works of references to antiquity or of the kind of folkloric images of Greece created by a number of popular films conflicts with what the English-speaking reader has come to expect. […] A great deal of modern Greek poetry has been translated but it has failed to make an impact in the English-speaking world and contemporary Greek poets are generally conspicuous by their

absence from the shelves of English bookstores and from the international stage in general. (2003: 13; my emphasis)

Twenty years before Connolly wrote these lines, in the Introduction to their translation of Elytis's *Selected Poems*, Edmund Keeley and Philip Sherrard noted 'Greek poets have been labouring under the shadow of their illustrious forbears, a circumstance that has either concealed them altogether or implied that they could not be recognised unless they conformed to an image that in many ways is totally alien to them' (1981: ix). However, two years after Elytis was awarded the Nobel Prize for Literature, the same two translators had reason to be optimistic: because of a new wave of translations, whereas thirty years previously, '[...] poets like Solomos, Palamas, Cavafy, Sikelianos and Seferis were all but unknown outside Greece, and this in spite of the fact that their work for the most part was completed during the first half of this century and in the case of Solomos well over a hundred years ago' (ibid.). As for Elytis's own perspective, this is featured in the same Introduction, through excerpts from an interview with Ivar Ivask in *World Literature Today* (1975), where the Greek poet precisely addresses some of those expectations. He tells Ivask how he has avoided classical imagery and myth, because of the artificial role that had been assigned to them in the post-Renaissance literature of Europe:

> I have never employed ancient myths in the usual manner [...] No doubt it is advantageous for a Greek poet to employ ancient myths, because he thus becomes more accessible to foreign readers. [...] I have reacted against this, often quite consciously, because I thought it was a bit too facile. [...] Since my chief interest was to find the *sources* of the neo-Hellenic world, I kept the mechanism of myth-making but not the figures of mythology. (Elytis, qtd. in Keeley and Sherrard 1981: xii)

What is more, within Greek poetry itself, relationships between past and present can be highly complex. Not only are felt continuities in the culture maintained over extremely long periods, but the diachronic richness underlying the modern language is often immediately evident to the native speaker, so that ancient texts can be understood, at least to some extent, even without the help of intralingual translation. While such levels of connectedness can hardly be said to function between Old, Middle and

Modern English, in Greek, the multiple 'layerings' of language surface with far greater ease and considerably more varied consequence. Indeed, despite the caution of Elytis and others, contemporary poets often pursue analogies with the aid of a whole cast of characters from both historical antiquity and myth, along with aphorisms and dicta that are directly attributable to ancient sources. That is to say, an entire range of internal recognitions can be relied on to be more or less readily available. Non-Greek readers, however, who may feel the need to pay close attention whenever the adjective 'Greek' is announced, may also be liable to anticipate references and forms that are not necessarily present in any consistency in a poetic text, or at least, have not actually been grouped prominently. From the outside looking in, certain appropriations of Greece and Greekness have long taken hold on readers, often combined with the pervasive and lasting influence of cinematic representations, which in turn tend to militate against an 'uncontaminated' hearing. Inevitably, any such assemblages of voices, which are often disparate, themselves bring their own sets of problems. Before 2010's *The Greek Poets*, a previous large-scale project directed at an English readership took its cue from the millennium, and proceeded, over the course of 1024 pages, to limit itself to only *A Century of Greek Poetry 1900-2000* (Bien et al. 2004). And even though one of its reviewers, Dimitris Tziovas, found the volume successful not only in 'presenting a panorama' of Greek verse in the twentieth century but also in introducing several unknown voices to a wider Anglophone readership, he could not help questioning the usefulness of such publications in general, asking whether

> [...a]nthologies are still the best way to introduce the literature of a country to a foreign audience. And from this overarching question, others flow: whether to include fewer poets with a larger number of poems, or more poets with fewer poems; is a thematic arrangement preferable to a chronological one? Can themed anthologies such as the recent one on Greek fantasy writing (*The Daedalus Book of Greek Fantasy*, edited and translated by David Connolly, 2004), appeal more to an international audience? Indeed are anthologies popular with the general public or simply intended for an academic audience? (Tziovas 2005: 408)

Another anthology, *Austerity Measures: The New Greek Poetry* (2016), edited by Karen Van Dyck, not only responds in several ways to concerns posited by Tziovas, but also confirms them. This book, which is 457 pages long, includes forty-nine poets, most of them writing from the first decade of this century. Featuring selected poems in the original Greek, the volume provides an interesting exercise in contextualising current and developing work, by focusing on an overarching proposition: that sociopolitical strife concentrates the creative spirit. Van Dyck also finds herself wondering whether the poets should be ordered alphabetically, chronologically, around themes, or according to the influences that work upon them. She suggests that some organisation is required, 'not least because many of the poets are making their first appearance in English and will be unknown to most of this book's imaginable readership' (Van Dyck 2016: xx); and she concludes that a division into venues of poetic activity is more sensible. For this reason, she arranges her material in categories such as: 'DIY and Small Press Poets', 'Poets Online', 'Poets in Performance and across the Arts'. Crucially, this editor also realises the nature of the cross-cultural pollination that often enables these kinds of work:

> What most distinguishes the poetry of this new millennium from what came before it is, on the one hand, its diversity – there are no clear-cut schools or factions – and, on the other hand, the cultural conditions that it takes for granted. [...M]any of these poets have had ready access to computers and the internet since childhood. The reality they seek to represent [...] is infiltrated by, and includes, the virtual. They have grown up with the understanding that vast stores of information and a wide range of different languages are only ever a click away. Even those who have not been exposed to a mixture of languages in their own cities, towns, and villages, even those who have somehow missed it on the radio and television, have inevitably found it on their computer screens; and mother tongue, as such, often doesn't determine the language they choose to write in. Some publish in two or more languages; some self-translate. (ibid.: xviii-xix)

It is far from unprecedented that social upheaval, which is inevitably reflected in the culture, should be readmitted into our consciousness through metaphor and imagery. Yet it seems somewhat ironic that it should take a financial crisis combined with a comment on the cover by Yanis Varoufakis, a controversial economist rather than a literary critic, for a reappraisal of Greek poetry to appear from a prestigious publisher such as Penguin. It remains to be seen how many of these poetic voices will extend their presence in English beyond this current frame. At this stage, the results are admittedly uneven, and financial infamy post-2008 presents a different set of problems, often in the guise of 'opportunities': Van Dyck is certainly not alone in sensing that the crisis may help with a new situating of Greek poetry. A few months earlier, an anthology edited by Theodoros Chiotis appeared, bearing the title *Futures: Poetry of the Greek Crisis* (2015). The editor, as well as the translator, carries immense responsibility in cases such as these: the line between recording actual developments inside a literature and magnifying certain symptoms, titles and verses in confirmation of a sociopolitical outlook, or an agenda, can be very thin. Chiotis himself seems to be aware of this risk and even warns against it in some of his comments – even though his approach may well indicate an ambivalence that could appear more inviting to certain critical narratives than others:

> It is probably fair to say that the interest of foreign readers for Greek literature has been ignited by the crisis but we should be very vigilant about this renewed interest and in what way it might be appropriated. This is a very crucial moment for contemporary Greek literature regarding its potential promotion to a non-Greek speaking audience; in fact, *this particular historical circumstance might be a once-in-a-generation opportunity for contemporary Greek literature to be diffused outside Greece.* [...] *it is therefore very important for all interested parties to rethink the cultural, social and political implications* of the translation of contemporary Greek poetry and what it might ferry across languages and cultures. (Chiotis and Rossoglou 2017; my emphasis)

These brief mentions of recent attempts to anthologise and present Greek poetry to an English-speaking readership lie well within our zone of interest. As has happened with key anthologies in the past, for instance, C. A. Trypanis's *Medieval and Modern Greek Poetry* (1951) and Keeley and Sherrard's *Four Greek Poets* (1966), lasting impressions of Greek poetic production have been engendered and further selections of poets and poems have grown out of them. What is more, the quality of translations also has close bearings on the ways in which influences are then negotiated by British poets – first and foremost, of course, *as readers*.

Equally, well-composed paratexts – and the patronage they often imply – should never be underestimated: readers can be assisted in registering differences in form, in the genealogy of 'voice', and in the varied ways in which this foreign poetry offers enrichment. The earliest readers are often themselves poets – and sometimes, as in the case of W. H. Auden, they are also those who take us closer to a voice like Cavafy's. The very first paragraphs of his Introduction to Rae Dalven's translations in *The Complete Poems of Cavafy* (1961) poignantly observe encounters and processes that have already taken place:

> Ever since I was first introduced to his poetry by the late Professor R. M. Dawkins over thirty years ago, C. P. Cavafy has remained an influence on my own writing; that is to say, I can think of poems which, if Cavafy were unknown to me, I should have written quite differently or perhaps not written at all. Yet I do not know a word of Modern Greek, so that my only access to Cavafy's poetry has been through English and French translations.
>
> This perplexes and a little disturbs me. Like everybody else, I think, who writes poetry, I have always believed the essential difference between prose and poetry to be that poetry can be translated into another tongue but poetry cannot.
>
> But if it is possible to be poetically influenced by work which one can read only in translation, this belief must be qualified. [...]
> (Auden 1961: xv)

The four chapters in this book often examine similar issues, especially in their focus on the ways in which such influences and dialogues may be possible, often in wildly different forms arising between two literatures, and between original and translation.

ONE

'The *Iliad* Suits You':
Christopher Logue's Homer – from *Patrocleia* (1962)
to the Posthumous Edition of *War Music* (2015)

1
The Troy That Modernism Built

> It is odd that Homer, in the thirteenth century, should have copied down the adventures of Sinbad – another Ulysses – and again after many hundreds of years have discovered forms like those of his own *Iliad* in a northern kingdom and a barbaric tongue.
> —Jorge Luis Borges, 'The Immortal' (trans. Andrew Hurley)

In 1959, the poet Christopher Logue arrived in London following a five-year artistic exile in Paris, with three collections of poems under his belt, and soon joined London's burgeoning anti-war movement. By then, the victors of the Second World War were mass-producing and testing nuclear bombs around the globe. This was also the year when he was approached by two classicists working for the BBC, Donald Carne-Ross and Xanthe Wakefield, to work on a radio version of an extract from the *Iliad*. What appears to have been an accident of birth started taking shape in his mind as 'my Homer poem'; until a few years before his death in 2011, he was still at work on what is possibly the greatest poetic rendering of Homer since George Chapman and Alexander Pope. In place of collections of poems, we were offered the *Iliad* in instalments. The last volumes to be published were *All Day Permanent Red* (2003), roughly corresponding to books 5 and 6 of the *Iliad*, and *Cold Calls* (2005)[1] which saw the poet – at age 80 – receive the Whitbread Prize for Poetry.

---

[1] These two volumes append themselves to the Faber and Faber edition of *War Music* published in 2001. This includes the first whole of *War Music*, where *Patrocleia* (1962; Book 16), *Pax* (1967; Book 19), and *GBH* [Grievous Bodily Harm], Books 17 and 18, come together in one volume, first published by Jonathan Cape in 1981. The 2001 Faber edition also includes the later additions *Kings* (1991; Books 1 and 2) and *The Husbands* (1994; Books 3 and 4). As published in 2015, *War Music* encompasses *All Day Permanent Red*, *Cold Calls* and the unpublished fragments from *Big Men Falling a Long Way*, to create a definitive edition. With the exception of references to lines from the later volumes, I am quoting here from this posthumous edition. (All other poetry by Logue comes from the 1996 Faber and Faber edition of his *Selected Poems*.)

Extensively drawing upon Logue's memoir, *Prince Charming* (1999), several connections between the poet's literary output, his life, activism and views can be made, as these resonate throughout his re-creation. How verbal art coincides with personal narratives and a sense of creative autobiography is of interest here – especially when faced with a work that often comments on the problematic synapses between the realities of war and its aesthetic representations, its *music*.

This is also a work *of translation*: and in the Anglo-American context especially, there has been a steady flow of Homers. George Steiner, one of the first and staunchest defenders of Logue's approach to the *Iliad*, included fragments from the beginnings of *War Music* in the seminal collection of translations he edited in 1970, *Poem into Poem*. Later, in his essay 'Homer in English' (1996: 88-107), he observes that when it comes to Homeric epics it is sheer numbers which are of course impressive, but also:

> [T]he quality and diversity of the long lineage of translators and respondents […] the complexity of modulation, the investment of vision which takes us from Lydgate and Caxton to *Ulysses* and [Derek Walcott's 1990] *Omeros*. It is not only on Keats that Chapman's Homer exercised its uneven spell. What might Dryden's projected *Iliad* have been had he persisted beyond Book I? I do not see what English epic poem after *Paradise Regained* – and how abundant Homer is in Milton – rivals the authority and narrative sweep of Pope's *Iliad*. There are persuasive 'domesticities', as from a Flemish interior, in Cowper's *Odyssey*, in his treatment of 'that species of the sublime that owes its very existence to simplicity'. Shelley's *Homeric Hymns* exhibit both poetic virtuosity and a close knowledge of Greek Lyric texts. What understanding of modern English and American poetry could set aside the translations from, the imitations of the *Iliad* and the *Odyssey* in Ezra Pound – that magical first Canto! – in Auden's 'Shield of Achilles', in Graves, in Robert Lowell, in Robert Fitzgerald or in that incandescent reading by Christopher Logue? (ibid.: 89)

Before we turn our attention to this 'incandescent reading', we may further register how integral a part Homer is in the development of English poetry: Chapman's 'fourteener' *Iliad*, in its excited licentiousness and proud neologisms, facilitates an English heroic couplet. Pope explores previous translations as he works on his own *Iliad*, taking liberties in capturing 'that Rapture and Fire' of the original. Indeed '[t]he Homeric sequence is an inventory of metrical means: we find in it alliterative verse, rhyme royal, Spenserian stanzas, heroic couplets, iambic pentameter, blank and free verse' (Steiner ibid.: 93-4). And consequently, renderings of Homer trace a maturation of translation as both literary enterprise as well as enabler of critical acuity, a task extended in time and requiring considerable research.

When, moreover, the subjectivity and priorities of a poet shape the identity of the translation, as with Pope, Chapman or Logue, we observe modes of translating that are distinctly literary in conception and execution, as opposed to more classically *responsible* approaches of, for instance, Lattimore (1951), Fagles (1991) or more recently, even Lombardo (1997) and Green (2015). Logue begins by boldly disposing of the epithets and repetitions abundant in the *Iliad*, a consequence of the oral formulae of its conception. He then proceeds by way of compression and amplification, eliminating or re-imagining scenes. By way of illustration, we could cite the end of Book 16, in Lattimore's relatively close rendering, then in Fagles's somewhat freer version, and the same passage in Logue's compressed, intense phrasing.

> "[...]When he stayed behind, and you went, he must have said much to you:
> 'Patroklos, lord of horses, see that you do not come back to me and the hollow ships, until you have torn in blood the tunic of manslaughtering Hektor about his chest.' In some such manner he spoke to you, and persuaded the fool's heart in you."
> And now, dying, you answered him, o rider Patroklos: "Now is your time for big words, Hektor. Yours is the victory given by Kronos' son, Zeus, and Apollo, who have subdued me easily, since they themselves stripped the arms from my shoulders.
> Even though twenty such as you had come in against me, they would all have been broken beneath my spear, and have perished. No, deadly destiny, with the son of Leto, has killed me, and of men it was Euphorbos; you are only my third slayer. And put away in your heart this other thing that I tell you. You yourself are not one who shall live long, but now already death and powerful destiny are standing beside you, to go down under the hands of Aiakos' great son, Achilleus."

He spoke, and as he spoke the end of death closed in upon him, and the soul fluttering free of his limbs went down into Death's house mourning her destiny, leaving youth and manhood behind her. Now though he was a dead man glorious Hektor spoke to him:

"Patroklos, what is this prophecy of my headlong destruction? Who knows if even Achilleus, son of lovely-haired Thetis, might before this be struck by my spear, and his own life perish?"

He spoke, and setting his heel upon him wrenched out the bronze spear from the wound, then spurned him away on his back from the spear.

Thereafter armed with the spear he went on, aiming a cast at Automedon, the godlike henchman for the swift-footed son of Aiakos, with the spear as he was carried away by those swift and immortal horses the gods had given as shining gifts to Peleus.

(*The Iliad of Homer*, trans. Richmond Lattimore 1990 [1951]: 205-6; lines 838-67)

'Now don't come back to the hollow ships, you hear? –
Patroclus, master horseman –
not till you've slashed the shirt around his chest
And soaked it red in the blood of man-killing Hector!'
So he must have commanded – you maniac, you obeyed."

   Struggling for breath you answered, Patroclus O my rider,
"Hector! Now is your time to glory to the skies…
now the victory is yours.
A gift of the son of Cronus, Zeus – Apollo too –
they brought me down with all their deathless ease,
they are the ones who tore the armor off my back.
Even if twenty Hectors had charged against me –
they'd all have died here, laid down by my spear.
No, deadly fate in league with Apollo killed me.
From the ranks of men, Euphorbus. You came third,
and all you could do was finish off my life…
One more thing – take it to heart, I urge you –
you too, you won't live long yourself, I swear.
Already I see them looming up beside you – death
and the strong force of fate, to bring you down
at the hands of Aeacus' great royal son…
              Achilles!"

Death cut him short. The end closed in around him.
Flying free of his limbs
his soul went wringing down to the House of Death,
wailing his fate, leaving his manhood far behind,
his young and supple strength. But glorious Hector
taunted Patroclus' body, dead as he was, "Why, Patroclus –
why prophesy my doom, my sudden death? Who knows? –
Achilles the son of sleek-haired Thetis may outrace me –
struck by *my* spear first – and gasp away his life!"

With that he planted a heel against Patroclus' chest,
wrenched his brazen spear from the wound, kicked him over,
flat on his back, free and clear of the weapon.
At once he went for Automedon with that spear –
quick as a god, the aid of swift Achilles –
keen to cut him down but his veering horses
swept him well away – magnificent racing stallions,
gifts of the gods to Peleus, shining immortal gifts.
  (*Iliad*, trans. Robert Fagles 1998 [1990]: 440-1; lines 980-1017)

You and your marvellous Achilles;
Him with an upright finger, saying:
  *"Don't show your face to me again, Patroclus,
Unless it's red with Hector's blood."*
  And Patroclus,
Shaking the voice out of his body, says:
  'Big mouth.
Remember it took three of you to kill me.
A god, a boy, and, last and least, a prince.
  I can hear Death pronounce my name, and yet
Somehow it sounds like *Hector*.
  And as I close my eyes I see Achilles' face
With Death's voice coming out of it.'

  Saying these things Patroclus died.
And as his soul went through the sand
Hector withdrew his spear and said:
  'Perhaps.'
    (Christopher Logue, *War Music* [*Patrocleia*] 2015: 249)

If, for the moment, we take the Lattimore, or even the Fagles, to stand for the original, the extent of deviation in Logue's version is quite clear, even as he keeps the essence of Patroclus' final moments in the shadow of Hector. What reaches us is a 'dreamworking' of Homer, an evocative *processing* of an original that presents us with the translator-as-editor, abstracting from his primary text and distilling its essences, intensifying his understanding (and ours) through visual collages and cinematic language. It is certainly difficult to describe the textual outcome more succinctly, though there have been sporadic attempts (Willis Barnstone's taxonomy of literary translational approaches in *The Poetics of Translation* (see 1993: 25-30) defines Logue's project as a newly structured, 'uniquely literary' metaphrase). But this is how we gradually arrive at 'Logue's Homer', as proudly stated on the black cover of the 2001 Faber edition: the added possessive, as with Chapman and Pope before him, makes and unmakes both Homer and Logue.

As the previous paragraph suggests, Logue as a poet-translator owes much to the precedent of Ezra Pound, who establishes the aesthetic priorities of literary modernism also through works like *Cathay* or *Homage to Sextus Propertius* (J. P. Sullivan (1965) practically invents the term 'creative translation' in describing what Pound does). Logue shares Pound's principles, particularly in that *War Music* appears conceived 'as a series of "brilliant moments", both at the level of the individual phrase and in its overall architecture' (Underwood 1998: 61). As Josephine Balmer informs us, it is only after close attention to Carne-Ross's 'On Homer' tutorials and to the previous translations of the *Iliad* that this *War Music* starts being heard, that Logue 'began to break free, like an abstract painter building out from initial figurative studies, following new narratives, paraphrasing dialogue, guided only by Johnson's dictum that the merit of a translation can be judged by its effect as an English poem' (Balmer 2003/2004: 79).

In his introduction to *Poem into Poem*, Steiner already recognises that 'the contemporary translator and even reader of classic verse comes after Pound as the modern painter comes after Cubism' (1970: 34), and points us further to deployments of translation as originating in a 'contrary force' that has been at work 'in the modern sensibility: a hunger for lineage, for informing tradition, and a simultaneous impulse to make all things new' (ibid.: 31). Translating is seen as part of the poetry, certainly much more than an exercise in apprenticeship; it is legitimised as a literary mode that serves to extend central preoccupations with gender, politics and language. From the first pages of his compelling study of *Translation and the Languages of Modernism*, Steven G. Yao (2003: 2) recognises that Pound was 'the first broadly influential writer since at least the seventeenth century to bestow upon translation (over and above merely so-called original composition) an explicit and generative, rather than a derivative and supplementary, role in the process of literary culture formation'. Yao extensively argues that translation has been midwife to – if not often coincident with – literary innovations that paved the way for the trans-lingual poetics of *The Cantos* or *Finnegans Wake*, as modernist authors proceeded to redefine and augment its operative parameters. This also corresponds with a distrust of scholarship in the sense of removing literary translation from the realm of non-poets (scholars, critics). As Yao, among others, reminds us (see ibid.: 10-15; also, Yao 2010), Pound perceives his lack of knowing Chinese as a decided advantage rather than a hindrance; it might paradoxically enhance overall understanding. Full comprehension of the source language is not a formal requirement for an influential translation. (Note how Logue can mirror Pound in those respects, in his introductory comments to *War Music* as well as across the interviews he has given; see also Underwood (1998: 56-61) on Logue's animosity towards scholar-translators). Pound himself, in a well-known essay on translating Cavalcanti, reminds us of the various ways he begins to move from, in his words, 'the crust of dead English' (1992: 85) to versions that show the reader 'where the treasure lies' (ibid.: 92). He eventually synchronises thirteenth-century Italian verse with pre-Elizabethan English and, for Lawrence Venuti, he fashions in fact a 'stylistic analogue' that 'recontextualises both poetries with a modernist difference, laying the groundwork for their reinterpretation and revaluation' (Venuti 2013: 171). This example extends to several other projects, most poignantly in the *Homage to Sextus Propertius* (1919), where we note further disregard of prerequisites of closeness to original (and its language) in favour of re-energising, re-contextualising it: finding relevance for the present, designing dialogue between poets as translators, and using linguistic distances as a springboard for formal experiment.

At the same time, the translator's subjectivity is seen as integral in terms of what is said through a transformed original. There is more recycling and embedding of previous art, a method of translation as quotation; often part of a multilingual mirror that serves to suggest a contradictory and refracted modern consciousness. As we will see in the following chapters, imitations increasingly enter poets' collections, often so dramatically as to turn some of those books into cross-sections of the workings of influence. More than before, we are invited into the mind of the writer as s/he processes other literature.

It is hardly an accident that such awareness concurs with a reconsideration of the terms that portray alchemy or synergy between sensibilities: among others, a 'version', an 'homage', an 'excavation' even (as we shall see in the case of Alice Oswald in the following chapter), and, to return to Logue, an 'account'. *War Music* describes itself thus in relation to the *Iliad*, yet its poet has always been a willing participant in the definitional confusion – imitation or metaphrase, adaptation or new poem? – surrounding what he does as he inserts parts into the whole: *Patrocleia* (1962) is 'freely adapted into English'; and *All Day Permanent Red* announces itself on its title page as 'the first battle scenes of Homer's *Iliad* rewritten'. Tensions relating to naming also reflect an essential symptom of poetic translation: with respect to the ensuing formations or hybrids, it is mostly fluid descriptions of a distinctive approach that prove feasible, rather than exact designations.

Given Logue's early alignment with Pound and Eliot, and the reverberations of modernism in his original poetry – which become more obvious as he explores the variants of poster poetry and performance poetry during the 1960s – it is hardly surprising that he awakens to *War Music* as a neo-modernist work-in-progress. Yet subscribing to these aesthetics involves a notorious legacy: as modernism gained momentum in its brutal confrontation with past and present, it compelled Wyndham Lewis to state that it was astonishing to find 'how like art is to war, I mean "modernist" art' (1937: 4). For Marina MacKay, pronouncements like Lewis's really show 'how soon after the heyday of high modernism attempts were already being made to historicize literary experiment in relation to war' (MacKay 2017: 14). A host of precarious ideas was accommodated as aesthetics and politics mingled in the course of the First World War, and as the prospect of a second one loomed. In *Writing War in the Twentieth Century* (2000), Margot Norris suggests that as modernism proceeded to replace representation with performance, its

> self-reflexive pre-scription of the war as (energetic) formalism may thus have colluded in the phenomenology of the Great War by placing the mass dead's irrational and illogical production under an erasure that itself pre-scripted and, in a sense, pre-dicted World War II. (ibid.: 35)

There is no overstating how vocal artists and movements had become at various points during that period: the whole of Norris's first chapter is of interest, where she reflects on the impact of statements such as the 'we will glorify war – the world's only hygiene' of Marinetti's Futurist Manifesto. Logue's stated endeavour of conveying Iliadic morality in *War Music* on the other hand, could invite criticisms of sensationalising violence. His intentions certainly, are different, and he famously holds Eliot accountable for anti-Semitic nuances in a much-publicised correspondence in the *TLS* (for his reflections on this see Logue 1999: 214-15). Elsewhere, he is indeed all too aware of the pitfalls that led to Pound's fascist salutes and post-war adventures:

> [...T]he texts of the radio broadcasts Pound made to the American soldiers who were fighting in Italy in 1943 and 1944 [...] were worse than I had guessed. Full of anti-Semitic ravings [...] Pound was a fighter for the kind of literary art I admired, an experimental idea of beauty. And at the same time, he was advocating a perverse delusion realized through a criminal ideology.
>
> Literary commentators who try to justify, or apologize for, racist – in Pound's case – views by appealing to the poet's undoubted gifts soil themselves. In verse (as elsewhere) beauty will serve any view and give it a glamour. We should not be afraid to call it whorish. (ibid.: 152)

Logue's project should also be evaluated alongside his political outlook and perspectives on artistic endeavour. Most of his work, not least his overtly anti-war protest poetry of the 1960s, confirms a firm belief in poetry as a force for change; the poet has always been 'strongly committed to an idea that poetry should play an active part in society' (Logue 2003b: 125). In interviews and at several points in *Prince Charming* (1999), there is a certain accountability at the back of his mind while he is translating Homer; this new *Iliad* will reset some of the encodings of modernism to another, more responsible, socio-ideological agenda.

2
Paint it Red:
Between Logue's Early Experiences and an 'Account'

Logue's memoir shows how his formative years were marked by military, political and ideological battles. The book starts with recollections of Britain entering the Second World War (1999: 39-44) and moves towards his prison spell in 1961 for 'civil disobedience', together with other members of the Committee of 100, the anti-war group against atomic weapons, led by philosopher Bertrand Russell (ibid.: 265-77). Between these two demarcating experiences, we find a restless and confused young man keen to escape and perhaps join 'the army commandos from where it was a short step to strange units such as Popski's Private Army, among whose heroes I imagined myself' (ibid.: 46). In 1944 he volunteered for the Black Watch, and began a stint with this Scottish regiment as part of the British presence in what would soon become Israel. There he witnessed the onset of a conflict that was to have a strong and lasting effect on him; and attempting to dispose of some ill-advisedly taken army paybooks, he landed himself in a Palestine military prison for theft (ibid.: 58-74). During this whole period, Logue not only acquired a soldier's practical understanding of the realities of the military way of life, but was able to reflect on and study the deeper causes and consequences of the Middle Eastern conflict and gradually, of wars in general. In the sixteen months he spent in prison, he continued to write poetry, an activity that had first started in earnest in army camp libraries. The image is a striking one.

Logue's verse – direct, declamatory and combative – fittingly begins by drawing on his early experiences as a serviceman, and soon becomes preoccupied with the inherent absurdities of human nature and the irrationality of war. This is more evident in poems such as 'Loyal to the King', 'The Song of the Imperial Carrion' and 'The Song of the Dead Soldier' (see *Selected Poems* 1996: 14-15, 16-17 and 26-27 respectively) which recount first exposures to military exploits – the latter begins with 'For seven years at school I named / our kings, their wars (if these were won)' – and take note of political betrayals as well as patriotic loyalty. Throughout his writings, the poet often resorts to military lexis in articulating political protest and societal discord. Before work began on his 'Homer poem', characters and analogies from the *Iliad* are considered, and with hindsight, a reader is able to trace Logue's poetry gradually towards a 'shared concern'. When *War Music* starts happening, the poet-translator becomes both 'host' and 'guest'. We are quickly reminded of Charles Tomlinson's insight that in the best translations, 'there is an area of agreement between translator and translated, something they have spiritually in sympathy' (2003: 26). The *Iliad* comes to affect Logue's poetic stance as his voice tries to find sources for itself; at the same time, the poet, welcoming the prospects of concentration and annexation, starts to *infect* the ancient epic with his own staccato syntax, laconic rhythms and eye for irony.

In his Paris years, Logue's views on a fairer, classless society became stronger and more articulated. His concerns at this time extended to the moral power and social responsibility of art and of poetry, which, however avant-garde, cannot be above politics (see 1999: 160-1 and 190-7). Then, Logue's youthful, anarchic, left-wing enthusiasm was exposed to the anti-nuclear movement in London. At this time of Cold War, he was wary of what he and others perceived as a misguided Western defence policy and became convinced that a significant minority of intellectuals, 'blessed with the power of detached, informed, analysis fails in its duty if it fails, when necessary, to criticize, as well as to support, the institutions that sustain it' (ibid.: 229). He was thus quick to join the Campaign for Nuclear Disarmament (CND), which culminated in the Aldermaston March of 1958. He was part of what Alan Sinfield in *Literature, Politics and Culture in Postwar Britain* calls the 'rise of left-culturism', rooted in liberal humanism and disaffected with the policies of the prevailing system (see esp. 1997: 232-77). At one of the regular meetings held before the march itself at the house of critic Kenneth Tynan, Doris Lessing, who had recently been reading the *Iliad*, suggested to Logue that it 'suited' him (Logue recalls her saying it was '[s]omething to do with heroism, tragedy, that sort of thing', 1999: 221). According to the poet himself, this suggestion was made only days before Carne-Ross proposed the BBC version.

It is not hard to see why others recognised certain connections; and if the artists and writers involved in the anti-war group required a 'model' for the brutal lessons of history, a sounding board for their own stance towards it, the *Iliad* perhaps fitted this purpose. Already, Logue's inclination to versioning enables the political charge of his poetry, be it a Brechtian-style pastiche of the anti-nuclear lobby ('To My Fellow Artists', 1996: 28-32) or a chorus from *Antigone* on man's propensity for confrontation: 'We long to destroy the things we have made / Finding no enemy, we become our own enemy. / As we trap the beasts, so we trap other men. / But the others strike back, trap closing on trap' (ibid: 6-7).

Logue's frequent public readings, and the speech-act immediacy of his poetry, in fact shape his attitude to Homer. This will also be a translation 'for the many'. Its stimulating visual configurations notwithstanding, *War Music*'s greatest asset, arguably, has to do with going back to the beginning, to a long-lost oral tradition, gathering us around what is spoken; Logue's incremental re-writing is, at the same time, a re-oralising. In this sense, it is not surprising that the poet feels that work on the poem 'does not end with the manuscript. For me, until I have heard it read aloud, the published text is incomplete. I made a lot of changes to the text of *Kings* after hearing the BBC Radio performance' (1993: 256; see also Christopher Reid's notes in section 4).

And yet, the poet begins to doubt the sincerity of his political commitment when he finds himself in prison once more with others of the Committee of 100. He reflects on what he understands as naiveté in some of his views. This is perhaps matched by his innocence when first confronted with the Iliadic world: initial impressions, such as that of Achilles as 'some kind of a Nazi', are patiently countered by Carne-Ross and Wakefield's explanations that there are no 'good' or 'bad' characters for Homer (1999: 223); and that '[t]he Greeks are not humanistic, not Christian, not sentimental [...] They are musical' (ibid.: 209-10). These insights echo Rachel Bespaloff, in her classic commentary on Homer's epic:

> Who is good in the *Iliad*? Who is bad? Such distinctions do not exist; there are only men suffering, warriors fighting, some winning, some losing. The passion for justice emerges only in mourning for justice, in the dumb avowal of silence. To condemn force, or absolve it, would be to condemn, or absolve, life itself. (2005: 50)

A kind of reassessment accelerates as the poet is immersed in Homer's world. Logue's memoir notes, for instance, a powerful sentence in W. E. Gladstone's *Studies On Homer and the Homeric Age* (1858; qtd. in 1999: 274): '[I]f we cannot conceive of freedom without perpetual discord, the faithful performance of the duty of information and advice without coercion and oppression, it is either a sign of our narrow-mindedness, or of our political degeneracy.'

So, while core anti-war views and political positions will not change much, a wider complexity is gradually accepted. There are civic realities and facts that disallow the quick changes the young activist was once so fond of. Poetry should remain involved within society, yet the active political purpose of Logue's poetry is noticeably tempered as the poet realises 'how difficult it is to bring about a set of changes that won't make matters worse' (Logue 2003b: 126).

In this dialogue between original and translator, Logue's own views can evolve and mature, just as he increasingly realises that he is more creatively at home in *recomposing*, that is, in abstracting from what was before, than in 'starting from scratch' (see 1999: 223-4; other reflections on poetic translation in 248-9). Indeed, when discussing Logue's work, Matthew Reynolds believes it is the mode of work itself that largely propels the project:

> Throughout his 'Accounts', Logue's writing has been most taut when most sharply focused on an idea that more seriously is an idea of the *Iliad*: the weakest parts of the collected *War Music* are the passages of expanded or invented conversation. *What most energises his imagination is an endeavour to translate*; that is, to pursue his particular mode of the poetry of translation, zooming in on an 'idea' of the *Iliad* while also putting its veracity in question. (2011: 230; my emphasis)

In this embrace, what is essentially Homeric, the violent pre-humanistic tenor of the *Iliad* might only be truly retained by imaginative updating, by modern equivalences of 'that Rapture and Fire'. However, such Iliadic 'installations' in our present consciousness will have different effects, empowering recognitions of the absurd reality of what is still happening around us. As Logue tries to speak truth to war, the main hope he expresses for *War Music* is that it will make people 'very much aware that warfare is somehow endemic to human beings. It is hopeless. We must keep trying' (2003b: 125). Through the use of anachronisms or the foregrounding of occasional comment, his treatment of the ancient text will share understandings of where we still are, politically and psychologically.

3
Intertextuality, Anachronisms, Re-animations

One of Don Paterson's 'Fourteen Notes on the Version' (2006: 73-84) may help us understand how acts of translation begin to create, or extend, such possibilities (even as we comprehend how both original and translation, in our case, exceed the norms we usually have in mind):

> [...] unlike the poem in the source language, fixed for ever in the time and the diction in which it was written, the translated poem can be translated not just into the language but the *culture* of the age, whenever that culture deems it necessary. This strange anomaly – the fact that the translated poem can undergo continuous cultural rebirth, in a way denied to the original – raises the possibility that some poems in translation could, theoretically, end up being *more* central to a culture than that of the language in which they were first conceived. Either way, they demonstrate that the life of the text is not circumscribed by its original incarnation and the influence it may exert on other poems. Even if we believe all poetic translation a fool's errand, the original nonetheless offers a blueprint for a wholly new poem the target language would never have otherwise produced. (ibid.: 74-5)

Much of what Paterson suggests above connects to Steiner's positions cited earlier, and allows us to reflect again on the centrality of Homer's epics within Anglophone culture. Yet the non-fixedness of the *Iliad* as originary text (the case also with much of classical literature, especially oral poetry) seeps and echoes into the sheer duration of Logue's endeavour; it encourages it to arrive at that more expansive, dramatic scene of re-creation, as we have begun to sketch from the previous section.

The liberties Logue takes in the shaping of *War Music* were also prompted at the point of the poem's genesis by the necessity of an interlingual approach that sees the poet sifting through previous translations and word-for-word cribs rather than working from the ancient Greek original. It also allows for his work to resemble a translation of translations, a mosaic of influences and echoes, registering the textual distance travelled, the impurities and layers of reflection added in reaching, from antiquity, through (post-)modernity, towards the palimpsestic Homer of now. His recasting turns its attention from an ancient text that Logue cannot read, to all interpretations and similarities subsequently. In fact, the use of allusions and anachronisms turns to a conscious strategy, and at points rises to an intertextual collision of voices from many battlefields through the centuries, a perpetual mapping of relationships between literature and conflict, art and war. Logue's 'Notes' at the end of the final volumes especially (see 2001: 211-12; 2003: 39; 2005: 46; collected and corrected in 2015: 337-41) list several references in a text creatively aware of its genealogy: we thus encounter lines and turns of phrase extracted from previous translations of the *Iliad* as well as from poems and versions of modernist forebears such as Pound (from 'The Return' and *Homage to Sextus Propertius*) or H. D. ('I would forego'). Insertions such as Pope's 'I am full of the god!' (in 2003a: 28) also serve to remind us of the junctures when both warring and translating collide in poetry; together with modernist fragments, a lineage is implied, alongside a history of approaches to both classical literature and translation.

A significant second strand of allusions may be called 'militaria', involving excerpts from historical, autobiographical and literary accounts of conflict. In the course of Logue's 'Homer poem', we have the building up of a select bibliography of war: we encounter Napoleon's cavalry commander Joachim Murat I (see Logue 2015: 96), or John Erickson's *The Road to Berlin: Stalin's War with Germany* (1975-1983; see Logue 2015: 168), extracted phrases from (war) memoirs or snippets from Tennyson (the 'long bronze slope', ibid.: 134, is borrowed from 1885's 'The Charge of the Heavy Brigade at Balaclava', I.17). Again, the reason is perhaps because the 'original' that Logue is trying to get his head around is warfare itself as much as it is the *Iliad*. But, initially at least, lines like '[...] Ajax, / Grim underneath his tan as / Rommel after Alamein' (2001: 13) also had to do with the aesthetic needs of *War Music*, since by Logue's admission, he found original metaphors repetitive and unengaging (see 2003b: 130).

A gradual accretion of warlords, war writings and weaponry across time places emphasis on the actuality of what is never too far from us: in this past present, conflict coincides with intertextual reflection on it. Together with the use of anachronisms, such elements show Logue on his way to confirming Pound's definition of the epic as 'a poem including history'. Within what is also *a translation including history*, one often encounters autobiographical texts: lines from memoirs, and reported voices that are 'there', and appear to observe and relate to us a diversity of conflict settings. The poet thus injects splinters of subjectivity – together, inevitably, with their respective historical moments – from the seventeenth century battlefield of Edgehill and the trenches of the First World War, to the slums of Harlem. Those para-sites append themselves to the body of Logue's account; participatory echoes, expert witnesses.

Perhaps more urgently than in original writing, intertextual elements within poetic translation point to autographic imperatives of a reading consciousness. Previous (literary) experiences in what is an *embodied* practice of reading are activated, considered again, within what the poet-translator now co-authors. In *War Music*, we have at least one of Logue's own memories confidently inserted into the poetic text (see *Kings* 1991: 54), simply revealing him and his friends in the spring of 1961, observing people in the modern town of Skopje. This autobiographical fragment, employed to the effect of a simile, poignantly reminds us of the subjectivity rendering an original into a further poetic text, and again points towards what I trust is a latency of life-writing in many translations. (See Nikolaou 2006a and 2008); by 'life-writing' in the context of translation we would not simply isolate those – very rare – narrative interjections, recognisable snapshots of life's 'contents'; but an underlying drive to embed in a translation, aspects of one's relationship with language, in the shape of phrasal recurrences, intertextual traces and 'favourite words' that carry a private, empirical weight and reference: the felt lexical significances, however idiosyncratic, that exist in the reading mind. Behind the words of a translation we often sense cognitions where words, languages, emotions and experiences uniquely fuse together. Here is Logue himself, in his *Areté* interview:

> When I was very young, nine or ten, I had precious words. 'Coruscating' was one –which I found when I was reading my Dad's *Roget* [...] For ages I tried to get 'coruscating' in somewhere or other. It would never go in. Then, 60 years later, I'm working on a passage of *War Music* that involves a Möbius strip, and suddenly there's a legitimate place for 'coruscating', so in it goes. (2003b: 127)

As the modern poet also composes through read memoirs, historical accounts of war and poetries emerging from the battlefield, embedding them into *his* translation, such fragments also participate in a textual autobiography; a self-translation of Logue. They exist like an in-built reality check within his method. They help us realise that there was an actual Trojan war, while conveying both the horrors and history/

art-making capacity of conflict across time. Paradoxically perhaps, an intended effect from these snippets of text is one of immersion; but even as we are assisted in inhabiting the warrior ethic that Homer recounts, Logue simultaneously hopes we also share a certain disgust of his heroes' behaviour. Moreover, for him, '[…] even stronger than disgust, there is a kind of hopelessness. A kind of fatality. People get taken over by passions –whatever this means. I want people reading *War Music* to feel this could happen to *them*' (2003b: 123; Logue's emphasis).

Cinema is one of the methods in which this immediacy frames Logue's reworking throughout: a representative, universal visual language of modernity, matching the comparable reach of the ancient epic. The panoramas of Logue's hybrid poetry-as-cinema, its ceaseless and varied travelling and reverse shots, jump cuts and stage directing (the frequently occurring 'go there', 'follow', 'see if you can imagine how it looked'), is what ensures that we are directly involved as the poet casts the unflinching eye of a modern medium over ancient proceedings. Asking us to, for instance, board airplanes or 'raise your binoculars' Logue makes us voyeurs in the unfolding bloodshed and/or actors inhabiting his camera angles. Readers of this Troy are not allowed to dissociate themselves from the inter-activity of the confrontation they find themselves in. With no higher ground for both reader and translator (as also live action commentator) to occupy, 'we the army' will often be asked to inescapably join Logue and 'slip into the fighting':

> Go left along the ridge. Beneath,
> Greek chariots at speed. Their upcurled dust.
> Go low along the battle's seam.
> Its suddenly up-angled masks.
> Heading 2000 Greeks Thoal of Calydon
> A spear in one a banner in his other hand
> Has pinched Sarpédon's Lycians in a loop.
>
> Drop into it.
> Noise so clamorous it sucks.
> You rush your pressed-flower hackles out
> To the perimeter.
> And here it comes:
> That unpremeditated joy as you
> – The Uzi shuddering warm against your hip

> Happy in danger in a dangerous place
> Yourself another self you found at Troy –
> Squeeze nickel through that rush of Greekoid scum!
>   (Logue 2015: 167)

Thus we are escorted into battlegrounds of amassing armies amid the cries of their leaders, and left there to our own devices, with barely enough time to ponder the sheer inevitability of it all, willed to experience the gamut of emotions we are often unaware of within our shared psychological makeup: from the paralysing fear of death to the adrenalin rush of surviving by ending the lives of others.

Richard Eyre's reflections on the persistence of conflict and our ambivalent emotions towards it are of interest in this sense: his childhood fascination with war games, his love of 'the romance, the nobility, the extremity and the secrecy of war' (Eyre 2003), of war as test of character and a proof of life, was gradually replaced by recognitions of its futility, the waste and irrationality of violent conflict, and a certainty of its eventual abolition. Later in life, this optimistic credo begins to appear, as with Logue, like a 'colossal naiveté'; nothing seems to change. Eyre's 'voilà moment' comes while watching war reportage on TV:

> After hours of homogenised 'rolling news', of reports from vicarious combatants ('embedded correspondents') talking with knowing assurance of desert strategy, rapid dominance and friendly fire, and with prurient awe of bombs, mortars, missiles and tanks, I realised that all this is happening because in some atavistic way, most of us must have a desire for the rush of adrenalin, for the smell of napalm in the morning, an appetite for war indistinguishable from the one that fuelled my childhood passion for it: the great game, tin soldiers made real. In the story of mankind, war is the one unbroken subject. (ibid.)

Much of Logue's project parallels such insight, his method enacting this 'unbroken subject'. From the previously encountered Rommel, or the kings asleep 'like pistols in red velvet' to the Ilian sky's gleam described '[a]s when Bikini flashlit the Pacific' (see 2001: 124), *War Music*'s vast armamentarium of anachronisms essentially helps enunciate a sense of timelessness.

In *All Day Permanent Red* (2003a), the Trojan War's 'first battle-scenes rewritten', this approach finds, more than ever, its justification. Of course, the face of battle has been phrased before, notably in *Patrocleia*'s protagonist's lethal rampage and in the battle around Patroclus' corpse in *GBH*; but *All Day Permanent Red*'s sustained, autonomous onslaught, properly identifies the *Iliad*'s actual core. Here, readers become detached from any 'meaningful' narrative save the deadly advance of Hector and Diomed (Diomedes) towards each other amid inexplicable mayhem. In an insightful meditation on how the reality of the battlefield and mourning turns to memorial through art forms, James Tatum argues in *The Mourner's Song* (2003), that our imagined distance from war helps us disconnect the epic's gory bulk of near-clinical descriptions of injury and killing from the few and far-between tragic moments and narrative pauses, like the parting of Hector and Andromache or the meeting of Priam and Achilles. We normally tend to focus on these, as readers and in our critical descriptions, while 'blood and guts, in fact, mean everything' (ibid.: 116). Noting the *Iliad*'s inquisitorial descriptiveness of wounding, of how humanity and its protagonists really come to life at the point of death (and this is also central in Alice Oswald's approach, as we will discuss in the next chapter), and alongside wider considerations of art's willingness to reconstruct processes and points of dying (thus helping us give meaning to both life and death), Tatum relocates the poem's essence in the chaotic, gruesome presentness of fighting; it is from this that poetry, music, *has* to spring forth: '[p]oet's song and warrior's song blend into a single melody as Patroclus turns killing itself into poetry. With apologies to Wilfred Owen, who found poetry in the pity of war, war's poetry is also to be found in the killing' (ibid.: 119).

The expressive volatility of *All Day Permanent Red* seems to share and voice such recognitions. With Espiner (2006: 25), we realise that Logue has understood 'the importance of the visceral dramatic narrative complete with all its bloody, almost pornographic, detail. If the violence isn't present tense, it has the dramatic quality of an eyewitness account'. Not only do wounding and dying emphatically happen in an eternal present, but Logue's experimentations with allusions to a modern consciousness reach critical mass, as we read of armies that hum 'like power station outflow cables do', of 'Porsche-fine' chariots, of Diomed with 'as many arrows on his posy shield / As microphones on politicians' stands' (2003a: 9). These radical equivalences transport the relevance of what would be distant terrains and pre-humanistic morals into modern circumstance, enforcing instant recognitions. They also help collapse our perceived distances from war, while echoing its complex, less-than-innocent interface with artistic expression.

This version of the Trojan battleground is a centre that holds; enough to involve and embed readers in the drama. A cursory look at the inconsistency in transliterating the very names of main protagonists confirms this Troy as a scene of global conflict; those ancient Greek names are now abstracted into numerous nationalities – among others Thoal, Merionez, Gray, Boran, Chylábborak, Idomeneo. The brutal acts of this international cast acquire universal relevance: these characters are never far from home, never safely inhabiting Greek antiquity. Rather, they populate a place where, to borrow from Eliot, 'all time is eternally present', a porous battle plan invaded by mentions of Missouri, Iwo Jima, Castile, or Gallipoli, where snapshots of conflict across history come and go. Logue's work perhaps confirms Rachel Bespaloff when she argues that it is indeed impossible to speak of a 'Homeric world', in the same way one can speak of 'Dantesque', 'Balzacian' or 'Dostoievskian' ones. Simply because Homer's universe (and she feels the same applies to Tolstoy's) 'is what our own is from moment to moment. We don't step into it; we are there' (Bespaloff 2005: 72).

What ultimately underscores *War Music* as a whole is neither a glorification of war, nor overt protest or uncomplicated critiques of humans fighting humans. It is simply awe in the face of conflict's undeniable power to foster identity even as the individual is lost in battle formations, to create societal structures and civilisations as it drives them to obliteration. What Logue invites us to share is an understanding of the senses in which war defines our being, even while we – the poet-translator surely, if his CV is anything to go by – want things otherwise. The result, inhabited by spears, artillery shells and nuclear warheads must remain an 'account' in that it demands we confront ourselves with difficult knowledge; recognise, at the very least, our imagined distances from war.

4
Drafts and Fragments

As the publication history of the later *Cantos* forewarns, large-scale poetic endeavours extending over decades and attempting to contain the world risk remaining incomplete; aptly perhaps, ambition and sheer length parallel the human body, the poet's endurance. Eight years before his death, in his *Areté* interview, Logue already considered *Cold Calls* the penultimate instalment, and went over some details of a plan to compress the considerable remainder of the *Iliad* into a further book (with the title

Big Men Falling a Long Way, coming from his friend Kenneth Tynan's description of tragedy). This plan would demand at least an escalation of most strategies so far used, and probably radical changes in the mode of composition (see 2003b: 132-5). In the end, illness stopped Logue; *Cold Calls* was to be the last book, even though several pages of unpublished material were included in the 2015 posthumous edition of *War Music*, edited by Christopher Reid; indeed, as the latter points out in his 'Editor's Note' (2015: 297-302), the poet had no desire to abandon his ongoing conversation with Homer: 'The numerous plans and schedules of the work as a whole that he was in the habit of drawing up as a writing aid demonstrate that he had a sense, albeit a fluctuating one, of what was needed to bring it to a conclusion' (ibid.: 297). What is more, *Big Men Falling a Long Way* indeed 'would have subsumed the whole of *War Music* itself, adding both preceding and subsequent incidents [...]' (ibid.: 299).

This final iteration of *War Music*, then, involves not only corrections to both previously published editions and notes (Reid reminds us that Logue was a habitual, in fact obsessive, reviser of his work, so that even the edition published in 2001, 'had, in the three years before he dropped the Homer project once and for all, acquired, in the author's own copy, numerous insertions and marginalia that demonstrate his unresting dissatisfaction [...]' (ibid.: 300). Reid incorporates these changes, updates the notes and copiously sifts through all that was left behind by the poet now dead – and it is rather a lot, since

> Logue's method of composition means that notes, sketches, rough drafts, attempted fair copies – inevitably and immediately rendered doubtful by second and third thoughts – have proliferated promiscuously, all now vying for the editor's attention. There are dozens of MS pages which show the poet attacking this or that passage again and again, as if in the hope of knocking it into submission by just one final thrust. In addition to such abundance, the binders, folders and boxes that contain it contain much besides: synopses, also under constant revision; quotations from literary and ephemeral sources of different kinds; letters concerning work in progress, which may also include variant drafts or conflicting statements of intent; and more. All these, in the form of sheets from note-pads, pasted cuttings, photocopies, yellow stickies – even thriftily scissored yellow stickies! – share space with the supplementary material of which Logue was an avid collector: clippings from newspapers and magazines, for the

most part, on a surprisingly wide range of topics, any detail of which might ultimately be fed into the on-going, juggernaut-like *magnum opus*. (ibid.: 300-1)

The drafts and fragments included in *Big Men Falling a Long Way*, as an appendix to this definitive edition consist of scenes, between a few stanzas and a couple pages long, from Books 10, 12, 13, 14, 21, 22 and 24, as well as a couple 'unplaceable' fragments (ibid.: 309) left aside until they found their place in the whole:

> Take an industrial lift.
> Pack it with men fighting each other,
> Smashing each other back against its governors
> So the packed cage shoots floors up, then down,
> Then up again, then down, lights out, then stops,
> But what does not stop are the blows,
> Fists, feet, teeth, knees, the screams of triumph and of agony
> As up they go, then stop, then down they go.
> No place on earth without its god.
>
> [2]
>   Sunshine; far out at sea,
> Nothing except an aircraft-carrier in sight,
> A plane just landed on its deck,
> Its two-man crew loosening their helmet-straps.
>   Then, suddenly, but with no other change, there is a swell
> And so the surface of the water lifts, the flight deck tilts,
> The plane, and crew, slide overboard,
> And on the unruffled sea the ship sails on.

Reid explains their status, directly underneath (along with the process in which he works):

> These two isolated passages share a page with the heading 'Poss. Sims' – presumably 'possible similes', to be kept in reserve for some appropriate moment that never came. The first passage is almost entirely clean, with a single correction by CL himself; the second is the result of editorial negotiation between an initial draft in ink and CL's pencilled insertions. (ibid

In similar manner, various notes escort those fragments towards our imagination in the pages of the appendix. More than ever before, we are witnesses to a text that will never reach its exact intention, a less tentative shape than this; we must actively envisage what words could have been in-between. The poet at several points had warned his editors and readers what was to come ('there will be a whole section on Achilles' shield, which is a big deal in the *Iliad*. It reflects Homer's world. I'm going to try and reflect our world', 2003b: 134) yet this central, promised section is nowhere to be found among his papers. Nevertheless, Reid continues to process the existing material, warning us that his interventions may be frequent, based on textual evidence of course 'but carrying an unavoidable element of presumption with them' as he himself strives for at least a 'partial and impaired glimpse' instead of no glimpse at all, of this 'Modernist act of poetic reimagining and reworking' (2015: 301). As he painstakingly goes through the series of 'CONT.[inuation] PLAN' ring binders that Logue leaves behind, he decides on the text now seemingly stable in front of us through those crossings-out, deletions, try-outs we are also asked to imagine – his note following some drafts from Book 14 is telling:

> The bulk of the text here is taken from two pages of ink MS with pencilled corrections, some of the middle section duplicated, but with inconsistencies, suggesting two variant texts amalgamated in a spirit of makeshift. So this is an editor's best shot at reconciling the two. The final line is from a third page, a rougher sketch of the same incident. (ibid.: 313)

In many respects, the lines now in front of us become even more poignant thanks to instabilities which defined, though less visibly to us, text-production throughout those nearly fifty years. Even before we reach the further certainty of this essential 'non-fixedness' that Reid attempts to manage following Logue's death, it is an element not lost on *War Music*'s many reviewers: Elizabeth Cook, whose long interest in the poem is no accident given her own prose work, *Achilles* (2003), brings to readers' attention how this text was 'ever in creation: changing in the way that a living organism changes and in the way the *Iliad* must have changed and grown *in the mouths and bodies* of its first speakers' (2002; my emphasis). Similarly, in her review of *All Day Permanent Red*, Shomit Dutta (2004) argues that 'Logue's work questions the idea of a single, static poetic text.

[*War Music*] has evolved over 50 years and it consciously engages the more unstable oral tradition from which the *Iliad* arose'.

In this sense also, it is apt that *War Music* happens *in translation*, as well as incrementally. Logue's approach, moreover, serves to confirm Steiner's insight that the 'linguistic-cultural distance to the Homeric is both talismanic and liberating. We revert to Homer as, in some ways, an unattainable dawn and model. But we are sufficiently remote and free from him to answer back creatively' (1996: 105). The modern British poet's response to an ancient Greek epic tries to bring home many things; notably, without moralising. If nothing else, this 'account' rightly captures and communicates, once again, the essential: as Logue puts it (qtd. in Hoggard 2006: 25), 'the *Iliad* tells the truth about something very important: the propensity to violence in human males'.

Two

Translating as Part of the Poetry

1
Before and After Ted Hughes

Repeated appearances of ancient poetry and drama in English, particularly from the mid-1990s onwards, suggest a grasp at continuity; as we have extensively observed in the work of Logue, the engagement with classical literature may double as a search for more stable points from which to contextualise the present, or observe diachronies. To what extent do we still inhabit an Iliadic world? How many *Antigones* across history? In her essay, 'Variations of Translation', Susan Bassnett relays to us the sense that

> Richard Schechner's *Dionysus in 69*, staged in New York in June, 1968 and Ted Hughes' *Oedipus*, staged in London a few months earlier signalled a renewed interest in ancient Greek theatre, both versions being radical interpretations of classical texts at a time of considerable political instability. Since then, the mythic plots of ancient theatre have been taken up in other politically volatile moments, such as the siege of Sarajevo, the Gulf War, the conflicts in Iran and Afghanistan, and, very prominently indeed, in Northern Ireland. (Bassnett 2014: 61)

In Hughes's *Selected Translations* (2006), posthumously edited by Daniel Weissbort, we come across an extraordinary account of his process with (Seneca's) *Oedipus* – where he admits to 'discarding the ornateness and the stateliness' (Hughes 2006: 60), continuously shortening and stripping bare the text. There is, however, a brush with classical translation nearly a decade earlier, and aimed at a different audience, when the poet is asked by Anthony Thwaite to translate from Book V of the *Odyssey* (lines 382-493, 'The Storm'), for a series of programmes of verse translations from Homer for the BBC Third Programme. The editor of the *Selected Translations*, Daniel Weissbort, notes how well this seemed to fit with the poet's preoccupations: 'Everyman's Odyssey' was published three years earlier in a pamphlet, *Landmarks and Voyages* (the poem was subsequently included in 1960's *Lupercal*), and in an interview with Egbert Faas, Hughes offers a telling response on his being often characterised as a poet of violence: 'Who are the poets of violence? […] [Y]ou'd have to begin with Homer, Aeschylus, Sophocles, Euripides, etc., author of Job, the various epics […] [P]oetry is nothing if not […] the record of just how the forces of the Universe try to redress some balance disturbed by human error' (Hughes 2006: 14).

There are affinities felt as well as observed by others several decades before Hughes's name becomes indelibly linked with key works of poetic translation, in *Tales from Ovid* (1997), Aeschylus' *Oresteia* (1999a) or Euripides' *Alcestis* (1999b). The last two were published after his death, and see him return to translating for the stage, where his work pulls in contrary directions – even as he is always cognizant of economy in the text, of it being 'actable'. For instance, he's asked for an 'imaginative retelling' of Aeschylus by John Durnin, artistic director of the Northcott Theatre, Exeter, yet he does not take many liberties beyond deleting some parts and not attempting to reproduce metre (Weissbort in Hughes 2006: 125-6); in *Alcestis,* on the other hand, a lot is added, notably the speeches of Death (see Hughes 1999b: 4-7). Not only that, but this commission from the Northern Broadsides company, specialising in performances in northern English speech, allowed Hughes to submit a text that also existed as an investigation, through the Greek play, of a linguistic and literary lineage. 'He had often commented', Susan Bassnett (2011: 42) reminds us

> on how Yorkshire speech patterns could be traced back to Middle English in an unbroken line of heritage. Now, translating Euripides, he made a play that could be performed by modern vernacular actors, reshaping the conventions and the language to suit modern audience expectations and at the same time creating a work that had roots in an ancient English literary tradition. It is hard to see how this kind of work cannot be considered a translation.

Most crucially these publications arrive at a time where Hughes's position as a poet and translator, following the near-simultaneous publication of the Ovid versions and of *Birthday Letters* (1998), could not have been higher. Publishing strategies and cover designs very much reflect this, further amplifying a mode of sensibilities inhabiting each other. In both the hardback and paperback UK editions of *Alcestis*, we note that Euripides' name is barely visible; Ted Hughes's name grows even larger in the paperback version, possessing all the information around it.

Hughes is certainly not the first British poet to be extensively concerned with the translation of dramatic texts; nor the most inventive in terms of how an ancient text may be utilised and re-voiced. Among Auden's frequent forays into verse drama and opera librettos we find *The Bassarids* (1961), co-written with Chester Kallman and based on Euripides' *The Bacchae*. (Auden himself describes in detail the fascinating transpositions and intersemiotic decision-making involved, in one of his lectures included in *Secondary Worlds* – see 1968: 96-102.) And Leeds-born Tony Harrison has offered supreme demotic adaptations over the years, very much aimed at communicating ancient theatre to a wider audience. Harrison's poetry, too, as even a cursory glance at his output bears out – most recently, his *Collected Poems* (2007/2016) – resonates with often playful, always consequential, classical references. Hughes's work nevertheless, is a study in how poetic status decisively influences reception. At the stage these translations appear, an established identity and the nature of Hughes's own work directs our reading; it matters less how creative, how *poetic* the translation is. In fact Weissbort is at pains to remind us, throughout his notes in the *Selected Translations*, of Hughes's 'literalistic' approach: of Hughes's thorough use of cribs, the poet frequently admitting that not much more needs to be done than install some pace and rhythm in the text he has been handed.

It is an approach that also defined *Modern Poetry in Translation* in its first period; the highly influential magazine, now more than fifty years old, published its first issue in 1965 yet existed as an idea from the late 1950s. There is good reason, then, for talking about translation within the work of poets 'before and after Ted Hughes', as we contemplate an Anglophone context in the wake of Pound and Eliot (and alongside extended, unique projects such as Logue's). Instituting this British-based magazine fundamentally helped revise approaches to foreign poetry (including, in terms of our present focus, two influential Greek issues, in 1968 and 1999). Hughes's *Selected Translations* are rightly supplemented at the end with introductory texts excerpted from several key numbers of the magazine. Writing in 1982, Hughes reflects on his and Weissbort's ambitions:

> From the start we saw our editorship as something like an airport for incoming translations, an agency for discovering new foreign poets, and new translators, who then, if their qualifications were right, might pass inland to more permanent residence in published books. We had a general notion of making familiar to English readers the whole range of contemporary possibilities

> in poetry – in so far as translation can convey any idea of such things. We weren't beyond the hope of influencing our own writers in a productive way. (Hughes 2006: 204)

And a few sentences later, we are offered a glimpse into their thinking about points of contact and some long-held ideas with respect to translation:

> Since our only real motive in publishing was our own curiosity in contemporary foreign poetry, we favoured the translations that best revealed the individuality and strangeness of the original. This usually meant a translation that interposed the minimum of the reflexes and inventions of the translator […] We were happily resigned, that is, to all the losses sustained by the most literal translation of the verbal sense. This method can have some drastic results: where the original poem's centre of gravity, so to speak, lies in the verbal texture, the poem can easily disappear completely. (Pushkin is the famous case of how all-important the verbal texture can be). But 'the most literal' covers a wide range between denotative and connotative extremes. Ideally, we would have liked to see at least some poems translated with the concern for both extremes. […] (ibid.: 205)

Hughes goes on to say that translators who approached them with 'parallel equivalents' were treated with suspicion. In the years since, attitudes have certainly shifted; not least at *Modern Poetry in Translation* and as reflected in the work of editors who took the helm from Hughes and Weissbort.[1] Yet access to other languages and poetic voices in publishers' lists – or

---

[1] Cf. comments by poet and translator David Constantine, around the time he and his wife Helen started their editorship: '[…A]lthough *MPT* is certainly a magazine for translation, its chief allegiance is to poetry. Which is why we are inviting submissions of original poetry – in any language (though always with an English translation if the language is not English) – that has to do with the core and continuing interests of the magazine, which are (consonant with the world we actually live in): the movement of peoples, diaspora, exile, the search for asylum, the speaking of mother tongues abroad; and also (consonant with our understanding of the act of translation): metamorphosis, the shifting of texts, the changing of their shapes down the generations and across gender, culture, frontiers of all kinds. Aiming at that, we aim to have a part in the whole endeavour of poetry in Britain today. That endeavour, that poetry, seems to us very lively, various and democratic. We shall be in an alliance with those publishing houses who, for little credit and less financial reward, insistently publish translations of the poetry of elsewhere' (Constantine 2004/2005: 41). After five years (2012-2017) under the editorship of Sasha Dugdale, who took over from the Constantines, the magazine is currently managed by the poet Clare Pollard.

within individual collections of poetry – happens on a different scale in the wake of *MPT*, and far more inviting environments have resulted from the dialogues traversing its pages every few months. It would arguably be less likely to come across books like Christopher Reid's *For and After* (2003), a volume consisting roughly half and half of versions of other poets (almost thirty names feature, from Horace to Li Po to Valéry to Tsvetaeva) and original poems bearing dedications. In this context, however, priorities change; poetry and translation as organic processes, and the emotional correlations of both, become more visible.

Translation has already been a constant motif in Reid's poetry, starting from the influence of American poets in his first two books, when he was still identified (with Craig Raine) as part of the short-lived 'Martian School', to the pseudo-translation poems from the work of an invented Eastern European poet in the career-defining *Katerina Brac* (1985). In *For and After*, however, Reid's experiments with personae, excursions into imitation and homage form a setting where an 'after' closely follows an original or becomes a 'take' that ventriloquises Reid's own preoccupations, and a 'for' is often found to be emulating another poetic voice (to which it is sometimes dedicated). With Steiner, we may locate one reason for this project:

> [...P]oetic translation is not only a living spark, a flow of energy between past and present and between cultures (immersion, so far as we may experience it, in another language being as close as we can come *to a second self, to breaking free of the habitual skin or tortoise-shell of our consciousness*); poetic translation plays a unique role inside the translator's own speech. It drives *inward.*
> (Steiner 1970: 27; my emphasis)

'Inward' gives a name to an impetus – in the sense of self-alteration, enrichment or progression; also because the literary self always functions through such exchanges. For Charles Tomlinson, in *Poetry and Metamorphosis*, the poet-translator, in the act of 'making it new', is 'simultaneously re-living the past [...] through the language he inherits, through the masters he follows, through the myths which often anticipate his own themes and even his own life' (2003: 142). In volumes as self-aware of this situation as *For and After* is, we also reach realisations of reciprocity, communication, empathy, of giving and taking: it is such attributes and motives that we locate behind creative translation, translational experiment, translation as part of poetry (and a poetics). In

Reid's paratexts to *War Music* (see chapter 1: 36-9) we have already seen him poignantly going through Logue's papers; and reflecting a thorough understanding of what can be poetically achieved through translation. It comes as no surprise, then, that Reid's own reworking of the Sirens episode of the *Odyssey* in *For and After* is subtitled 'after Homer and for Christopher Logue'. The myths, the classical encounters, *are shared*.

Indeed, we observe Reid's shape-shifting voice worming its way in and out of other poets' skins towards a new polyphonic whole, a personal anthology charting the dynamics, possible tensions and hybrids between poetic and translational activity. In the process, we are repeatedly shown the boundaries between the dedicatory 'for' and the record of an origin and a reading ('after') collapsing. As far as the traffic of inspiration is concerned, poetry and translation can be both 'for and after'. Here, Steiner's realisation in *Poem into Poem* is more keenly shown to be true: 'Each time a poem is translated, initiating a new poem, the original finds new and active life in present consciousness' (Steiner 1970: 27).

Again, these attitudes are influenced also by the levels *above* the more solitary and disconnected work of writing: Reid's stint as poetry editor at Faber and Faber from 1991 to 1999, working closely with the likes of Heaney and Hughes, Paterson and Logue, very likely encouraged a steady flow of poetic translations from the publisher during that period. In turn, this contributed to a change in both publishing and reading biases surrounding literary translation; there has been increased movement in this area at Faber's, most notably perhaps from Simon Armitage, the poet whose forays into versioning in many respects allow him these days to occupy a position not unlike that of Hughes. A few years after the staging of *Mister Heracles* (2000) – a contentious version of Euripides' play – and over a weekend in the late summer of 2004, Armitage's version of the *Odyssey* was broadcast on BBC Radio 4. The script of this commission as it was published two years later bore the subtitle 'a dramatic retelling of Homer's epic'. A necessary emphasis emerges and informs the translator's choices here, with some ensuing complications: the speech of epic poetry, as eventually written down, does not readily coincide with what is deemed speakable in today's world. As explained in his Introduction, much of the *Odyssey* is written as narrated poem, so

> when characters do enter into discourse, it tends to be with formal speech, rather than what we might call dialogue. Faced with that situation, the role of the dramatist is to transform such narra-

tion into a series of conversations and exchanges, and to actualise some of its unspoken intentions by putting speech into characters' mouths. In other words, to get people to talk. (Armitage 2006: v)

Obviously, this already sets off significant adjustments to the original text, but Armitage proceeds to critique excessive modernising: he quips that this version is not 'set on a housing estate in Salford' (ibid.: vi). He trusts the power of myth to enable resonances without the translator having to ram analogies into readers' heads. In this Homer, we do not come across anachronisms that teleport past into present – yet the language is undeniably modern; the dialogues patterned on everyday speech and pursuing plausibility (to the extent possible). A brief of simplicity and speakability does not imply indolence when it comes to the workings and effects of language. In 'The Lotus Eaters' episode for instance, we hear some of these subtle discoveries of rhythm and sound, as Eurybates reports to his King, Odysseus: 'Such smoothness enters the mind. / Colours are endless and limitless.' To which Antiphus adds how he feels 'a vast, velvet pleasantness' (ibid.: 78).

Armitage's most decided intervention is the organising of the action into three parts and (with the last one occupied solely by events upon Odysseus' return to Ithaca), then subdivided into brief chapters that follow the action, with the titles (e.g. 'Odysseus and His Army at Sea' or 'In the Palace of the Phaeacians') serving either to locate us in place, or centring on characters' key actions. Towards the end of his Introduction, Armitage admits that he hopes the 'script' may have 'further life' as a piece of writing. His *Odyssey* might not perhaps be counted among the classic revisitings of the epic, but it can certainly be included in a body of work increasingly inflected by classical presences (note, most recently in 2017's *The Unaccompanied*, Elpenor and Tiresias entering a British social cliché such as 'Poundland', 10-11). It is worth mentioning in this sense that Armitage follows this by further translation work on the Anglo-Saxon *Sir Gawain and the Green Knight* (2007) as well as *The Death of King Arthur* (2012), before he returns to Homer with a theatrical treatment of the *Iliad* as *The Last Days of Troy* (premiered at London's Royal Exchange Theatre in the late Spring of 2014). Introducing the published version, we find the poet himself commenting, as Logue did before him, on the constancy of human nature:

At the time when this play will be premiered, many countries will be marking and commemorating the centenary of the First World War, with images of atrocities and questions of military morality high in people's minds, just as they were for Homer. Moreover, the channel or strait that runs from the Bosphorus to the Dardanelles or Hellespont continues to symbolise a political, economic, cultural, philosophical and religious fault line between east and west. In that context, the story of Troy is a blueprint for a conflict that rages to this day. Homer was also astute enough to know that although it is armies who go to war it is usually the individual psychologies of their leaders that send their people into battle. Prejudice, pigheadedness, petulance or just a momentary whim can result in the slaughter of millions. Nothing has changed. (Armitage 2015: vi-vii)

Publications like those discussed here feature covers and blurbs that reposition reader response and criticism towards a text we are more inclined to agree is an 'adaptation', a 'version' or 're-imagining'. In some respects, we may call these *curated translations*; the settings that are fostered encourage one's voice to be both captured and furthered through others.

Logue's creative re-conception of the *Iliad* depends on intertextuality; it also questions, through its process and presentation, a number of latter-day assumptions about the poetic text – especially through *War Music*'s emphasis on orality, and uses of the language of performance and cinema. Reading this work, and the translations of Hughes, Reid and Armitage, is to find further proof of what Eliot perceives as he introduces Pound's versions: 'Good translation is not merely translation, for the translator is giving the original through himself, and finding himself through the original' (1948: 13). With Hughes, despite his care as an editor of *MPT* to defend the foreignness of the text – which may have led to a 'literalistic' approach in his own practice also – it is again understandable, if not inevitable, that his work as a translator 'parallels his other work and can even be seen as signalling various turns in its development [...H]is immersion in Classical drama, and the translation or reworking of some of its most important themes, extended his awareness of the possibilities of the theatre, particularly of its mythic dimension' (Weissbort in Hughes 2006: x-xi). What also emerges through these books (and those of Josephine Balmer and Alice Oswald, classicists both, discussed in the next sections of this chapter) is a true diversity of translational approaches; a wide range of dispositions and tonalities as poets find ways in and out of the source material in an effort to re-energise ancient texts, to attach their words to contemporary cadence and frames. The result often confirms the idea of successful poetic translation as one where its maker performs 'a transmission of civilisation in the process of extending his own voice' (Tomlinson 2003: 27).

2
Fragment as Method: On Josephine Balmer

'What makes a translation faithful? What makes a poem original? Having worked on a series of classical texts – lost, disputed, fragmented, often requiring more reconstruction than translation – I wanted to explore such questions further', writes Josephine Balmer in her Preface to *Chasing Catullus* (2004a: 9). And sure enough, this series includes her translations of *Sappho: Poems and Fragments* (1984 and 1992) and those of *Classical Women Poets* (1996). In the Sappho project especially, incomplete originals force one to dig beneath the remaining words. In cases like this, as Diane J. Rayor (1990 and 2016) has argued, this is to become involved in processes of decipherment and re-assembling in which both scholarly-critical and more subjective elements are intensified. What begins as translation might arrive at reconsiderations of the borders of the translating act. Which is partly what is occurring in *Chasing Catullus*, that book of 'poems, translations and transgressions' appearing simultaneously with *Poems of Love and Hate* (2004b), Balmer's translations from the Roman poet. Here, versioning of classical texts (among others, Sophocles, Euripides, Juvenal, Propertius) is but one aspect of an intricate mechanism of meaning. Balmer offers such versions alongside originals in 're-imagining epic literature, re-contextualising classic poems, redrawing the past like the overwriting of a palimpsest' (2004a: 9). This work includes a range of interpretive positions,

> from straightforward translation to versions based on or inspired by an original, as well as what I have called 'transgressions' – versions which shamelessly subvert a source text's original intent or meaning. These source texts, too, are wide-ranging, including not only classical literature but other English translations and poems, as well as churchyard inscriptions, newspaper articles,

even estate agent's particulars, fusing the strategies of translation and 'found' poetry. (ibid.)

We are thus offered a hybrid work that also exists as a record of the manifold cognitions of a poetic consciousness, a defining example of translation as a creative act: when correspondences of memory and text make translation feel as 'an existential, rather than just a linguistic, matter' (Scott 2000: 249).

The interaction of autobiographical and poetic desires first becomes clear in Balmer's preliminary admission that *Chasing Catullus* is also a response to the death of her niece, Rachel, from liver cancer. Within the book's three main sections – 'Before', 'During' and 'After' – almost every poem works with those that precede and follow it in reporting, sometimes overtly, sometimes subtly, the story of the girl's illness and dying. This sense of life-writing is especially pronounced in 'During' (Balmer 2004a: 23-37), where the poems surrounding Rachel's death emerge as a chronology of loss; they double as diary entries, bearing dates and times, retaining the umbilical cord between text and empirical world. In this context, (classical) translation becomes a necessary language, providing us 'with other voices, a new currency with which to say the unsayable, to give shape to horrors we might otherwise be unable to outline, describe fears we might not ever had have the courage to confront' (ibid.: 9). We thus encounter those varied channellings of myth into contemporary circumstance. Homeric passages of Odysseus descending into the underworld can be given titles like 'Letchworth Crematorium' (ibid.: 50) in dealing with what can perhaps only be expressed indirectly. What is more, translation enables, and better articulates, inner dialogues and conflicting frames of mind: of interest is the poet's own example of a poem about her niece's funeral that is immediately followed by a reworking of a prose passage from Plato's *Republic*, 'implicitly questioning the validity of any poetic response to such a tragedy' (ibid.: 9).

She also reaches to antiquity for consolation. From the lines from *Medea* invading her reading of the present in 'Greek Tragedy', to mute, weaving Philomela doubling for Balmer (ibid.: 22):

PHILOMELA

One way or another, I'd have done it myself.

Let grief, guilt or prick-sharp shame
wear down my tongue to a bloody stump;
slit my own throat, sliced off my lips,
in case my traitor speech should shape this place again.

So now I weave my words with crimson thread,
pick out my stunted songs in sacking cords –
the music of the deaf, the music of the dead.
And my soul frays at the plan I start to trace;
homes blocked in by sex and strife and sword,
the husband dropped, wife I'll never make.

And my heart knots at the thought of kids:
they seem too soft, too sweet, too pure to stitch.

Juxtaposition, recontextualisation, border territories in which original and translation provoke each other, are also key to *The Word for Sorrow* (2009) though this time around, Balmer's methods reach for wider terrain and more communal concerns, focusing on weavings of life and text across (national) history. Her comments on the genesis of this book, first published in *Modern Poetry in Translation* (Balmer 2005: 61-8), are particularly illuminating with regard to events in the creative consciousness:

> One rainy spring day I was working on an initial translation from *Tristia* using the Perseus site's on-line Latin dictionary, when an electrical storm required me to log off. Turning to an old dictionary, bought at a village fete as a school-student, I noticed by chance an inscription on its fly-leaf which I must have seen many times over the years and yet barely registered: a name in faded ink and a date, early in 1900. Back online a few days later, I ran a search on the name, almost on a whim. The results were impressive: First World War documents and diaries relating to 1/1st regiment of the Royal Gloucester Hussars, posted to Gallipoli in 1915, to the Hellespont, near Ovid's own place

of exile and which, by coincidence, Ovid had just described crossing in the poem I was translating. Following link after link, more and more connections were revealed; old photos of the regiment lined up on Cheltenham Station just before leaving for the east, bringing parallels with Ovid's famous poem describing his last night before exile. The eye-witness accounts detailing the sickness, deprivations and dangers of the Gallipoli campaign in which 50,000 Allied troops and 85,000 Turkish soldiers died, reminiscent of Ovid's own powerful laments about his conditions of exile. And so *The Word for Sorrow* came about, versions of Ovid's verse alongside original poems exploring the history of the second-hand dictionary used to translate it. (ibid.: 60)[2]

Balmer's internet search poignantly suggests Eliot's 'mind of the poet', the connective sensibility that simultaneously locates and effects meaningful wholes; moreover, it is often complemented with an archiving of memory: note how the above passage transports us into a rainy spring day, recalls images of old books being bought, asks us to share flashes of epiphany. Such recognitions often emerge during translating, and simultaneously may urge us away from it, demanding freer forms and narrative presences. Balmer seeks and embeds others as her work progresses:

[t]here are other narratives too; the private writings – diaries, letters, photographs, even poetry – of British soldiers on the eastern front, many of which mention my dictionary's owner, as well as the testimony of his daughter with whom I've been in contact, all providing, like Ovid's verse, striking source material (2005: 61)

– and therefore, it is the experiential element, these instances of life-writing which further catalyse translation and original and become reflected in

---

[2] In revised form, some of these early reflections are again encountered in the paratexts for the finished work (for instance, the above can also be found in Balmer's Preface to *The Word for Sorrow*, 2009: xiii-xvii). In the course of this chapter, I am quoting, wherever possible, from those early notes – not least in tracing – chronologically as well – the movement of composition and the poet's thoughts on what then was still a work-in-progress. The reader is similarly directed to Balmer's blog (https://thepathsofsurvival.wordpress.com/josephine-balmer/) where the poet recorded key moments (including early drafts and titles, historical context and philological discoveries) while she progressed with work towards two books eventually published in 2017.

the hybrid that will ensue. Ovid now is diversely cut up, condensed or adjusted to modernity, and at the same time invades Balmer's creative process and poems. The Roman poet was, of course, no stranger to such tendencies, himself inclined to hybridity and re-voicing: in *Ovid's Art of Imitation: Propertius in the Amores* (1977), Kathleen Morgan reminds us of a corpus permeated by imitations of the styles of contemporaries and antecedents (not only Propertius, but also Ennius, Catullus, Virgil and Horace), parodies of Homer and epic narratives, appropriations and collages of classical myth and legend. In this, Ovid seems to anticipate more recent literary agendas – and the poetics of (post)modernism.

In *The Word for Sorrow*, as experience and creative process turns to meaning-making, it always interacts with framing, fiction, form: Balmer soon realises that in what must follow and reflect the connections she makes, '*narrative drive* would be the key; the poems and renditions had to spark off each other, to hold the *dramatic* tension between the two as each *story* progressed' (ibid.: 60-1; my emphases). Indeed, it is not just the story of Ovid in Tomis and analogies in a historical Gallipoli that are being shadowed, but, as Balmer admits, there is also a 'third story of discovery, the detective story running like an undercurrent beneath' (ibid.: 61). This 'detective story' largely overlaps with the poetic act itself; it implies a self-referential component arguably activated more quickly when translation is near – whether as (meta)textual practice or part of one's multi-literate or -lingual identity. Not surprisingly, we move closer to a telling of a creative consciousness that is also a translating consciousness; indeed, Balmer is 'keen to use the device of the dictionary and its parallel lives as a jumping-off point for other themes, other layers of narrative beyond a simple Gallipoli/Tomis equation, *as more and more poems explored the relationship of text to translation or translator to language*' (2008: 120; my emphasis). And the outcome can be lines such as those coming at the end of the titular poem that closes her volume. Here, impulses of self-expression and metaphors for translation come together; and life and drama are shown as imperatives of each other:

> We are all translating the same story
> search same words in same thesaurus.
> What drives us on, keeps us to our path,
> in every version is not gain but loss.
>   (2009: 47; lines 76-9)

The onset of *The Word for Sorrow* is a possibility of blending versions and originals in pursuing associations and analogies that will give resonance to constants of humanity. Balmer closes her comments on her then work-in-progress by saying that her efforts have to do with forging links between antiquity and modernity, with expressing 'the invisible lines that connect us to often surprising points in history, finding common ground in unexpected places, celebrating the common humanity that binds us, whether we live at the beginning of the first, the twentieth or the twenty-first century AD' (2005: 61-2). Translation is part of a process of turning this material also into a meditation on conflict: the found stories and real or imagined voices of British soldiers in a foreign land crosscut with Ovid's sorrows and agonies – which become in this manner, more tangible than ever:

> If on this page you detect some new hand, fresh script
> I have dictated, don't fret: for I am sick –
> sick, here at the end of the unknown world, half-dead
> (reports of recovery exaggerated).
> Here there's no rest-home, rations fit for invalid,
> no one with physician's skill in pain relief;
> no one to comfort, wile away convalescence
> with tall tales, no friend to sit in attendance.
> Stranded far away, thoughts of home creep up in vain
> But most of you, dear wife, so I mouth your name,
> whisper at shades, sigh at shadows: they take your shape.
> [...]
>   ('Naso Writes his Own Epitaph', 2009: 20; lines 1-11)

– says the Roman poet, but he is not quite alone in feeling intense pain; his own words are preceded by ones attributed to the owner of the dictionary, renamed here 'Geoffrey', that Balmer uses to translate Ovid:

> *Those of us who came back no longer walked*
> *with the living. We had felt Hades' breath,*
> *our hair turned grey in that sharp blast of frost.*
> *The Turks could drop their bleak propaganda –*
> *'today the flies, tomorrow the vultures'–*
> *now we weren't men but novice corpses.*
>   ('Knocking at the Door', ibid.: 19; lines 19-24)

The often hybrid poems evidence some key stylistic preoccupations, continuing from *Chasing Catullus*: precise phrasing, inventive alliterations that frequently overlap with compound adjectives; paratactic syntax and judicious use of punctuation that rhythmically propel the monologues as they accumulate into narrative. Yet for all the technical complexity and (inter)textual experiment in this second book, we keep discovering immediacies of emotion in ancient settings and registers that would normally appear elevated to us now. The poet is helped in this precisely by the language reflected in those more recent writings from Gallipoli – see, for instance, the routines of war relayed in 'Digging In' (ibid.: 23) – as 'letters' from the scene of this conflict parallel the cuts from Ovid's poetry. In the process, some utterances, such as the one that completes 'Naso Sees Action' (ibid.: 32), escape in timelessness and a sorrow shared by all those who find themselves away, or between war and its recording: even if his Muse still dances to the same old tunes, the anguished Ovid reflects,

> I write for myself, read to myself: what else can I do?
> To whom can I recite my verse? Who knows the steps?
> Who can hear the music, follow Latin syntax?
> Yet my work, at least, is safe in my own judgment –
> for those who cannot read can give no assessment.
> Many lines are inscribed although most are condemned –
> still I send them home in the hope you will read them.
> (lines 22-8)

How far from translation do we find ourselves? Someone who wants to read Ovid's isolated voice will need to look elsewhere. In fact, Balmer herself mentions in her Preface Peter Green's 1994 translations of the *Tristia*, as filling that role, and admits that even at an early stage, the plan was to create versions towards a poetry collection (see 2009: xv). *The Word for Sorrow* goes beyond even that intention, offering a new composition, one that still includes the aim to *enliven* the ancient text; to appreciate and feel anew the reality beneath it. As a wide range of textualities alternate, inflect or appropriate one another in the 2009 book, translation is never far from creative negotiations and experiment; in fact, it enables a process from beginning to end. As Balmer reminds us,

> [t]he guiding force here, as ever, is *fidelity*. I start by working in detail on the text, poring over commentaries and scholarly

studies, weighing up the various theories and arguments, the prolonged discussions over every nuance of the Latin, to produce in the first instance faithful, literal translations. Only then can versions be shaped, like an abstract painter, perhaps, using figurative sketches and constructions as a basis for refining image into pure form or colour. (2005: 61; my emphasis)

And then those versions combine with, or are subsumed by, original or found poetry towards a story which again works through contrast and juxtaposition: the three parts of the book ('The Journey Out', 'Landed', 'The Way Home') track situations and persons, Ovid and the soldiers (and the poet herself) across time-frames and place-names. Translating is involved in an essentially modernist approach: some of Ovid's poems and lines may be accurately enacted but, as Balmer's own notes clearly indicate, many poems 'represent shorter, more impressionistic visions of their source text' (2009: xv). Then, far more cases are 'based on' or 'edited from' *Tristia* – not least because Balmer, as she informs the reader in her Preface, also intends the Ovid poems to seem 'like pages from a translator's notebook, detailed sketches before the finished original; to present snap-shots of a work in progress' (ibid.: xvi).

What is more, the classicist does not really go away; it is an identity informed by new insights gained in acts of poetry, just as the poetry also owes to understandings enabled by scholarly work. Balmer's 2013 monograph, titled *Piecing Together the Fragments: Translating Classical Verse, Creating Contemporary Poetry* focuses systematically on this dialogue, as witnessed especially in the writing and uses of 'explicatory translator statements'. She notes early on that despite such statements being viewed often with suspicion – as potentially unscholarly, or overly subjective, when it comes to classical texts especially – a more complete sense of the translator as also a writer in recent years means that such statements are beginning to be seen 'as an integral part of our corpus of translated literature; as invaluable primary sources for the ways in which writers, and particularly poets, have interacted with classical texts over the ages' (Balmer 2013: viii). She proceeds to survey how leading translators of classical poetry, from Cowper to Anne Carson, have written about their work, and integrates her own statements in what is shown to be a long tradition. At the same time, she expands significantly her own initial reflections – positioned, as we have seen already, as paratextual material or in essays in literary journals. In 2013, she is more able to analyse at length the process behind her translation of classical poets, along with the various ways in which such work is a branch of scholarship, and relies on the work of textual critics. Moreover there are also particularities of, or even contradictions in reception to consider. There are several cases which may suggest that 'the translator's task has become one of cultural as well as linguistic elucidation, filtering scholarly theories and new, contemporary ways of thinking about an ancient text for their new readership' (ibid.: 71). Yet in cases like Sappho's (and many of the lyric poets),

> if, as we have seen, classical translations are expected to be faithful renderings of the ancient source text, at the same time the conventions of contemporary poetry publishing demand that unreliable, incomplete fragments are presented in a form acceptable to their modern-day readership, as a rounded, accessible work of literature, usually without textual notes or other scholarly apparatus. (ibid.)

Of course, as already seen in several places in our discussion of Balmer's work, and as she again admits across comments on her own translations of Sappho and Catullus in *Piecing Together the Fragments* (see esp. 67-88 and 110-31), it is exactly those incomplete instances of text, the 'tattered sources', which inspire creative leaps. The further step of creating poetry, often based on this intense relationship between classical translation and research, is explored in significant detail in the latter part of Balmer's study (see ibid.: 156-89). She is aware of the movements taking place:

> following on from *Chasing Catullus*'s interplay between translation and original through extracts from a variety of sources, I now started to explore an interaction between translation and translator-as-narrator, this time based around a single source text, Ovid's *Tristia*. As I wrote of the work, then still in progress, in a paper for the 2005 Living Classics conference in Oxford, my aim was that: 'Here translation is not just a means of expressing or exploring the process of narrative but becomes an integral part of that narrative itself.' (ibid.: 201)

Such comment becomes even more significant as we consider work towards the two books Balmer publishes in early 2017. Even though we are naturally reminded of the twin publication of *Chasing Catullus* and *Poems of Love and Hate* in 2004, the implied dialogue offered now is quite different; not any more one between a book housing 'translation proper' and a volume dedicated to creative reassignments of classical material. Rather, both volumes belong in the latter category, and we are allowed comparisons of different modes so far achieved. In 2017, there is co-existence of devices and frames as developed from *Chasing Catullus* through to *The Word for Sorrow*. However, we should note, with Balmer, that there are already points of contact between 2004 and 2009 with respect to methods and concerns:

> [...E]ven as my narration as translator/protagonist reached its conclusion, as in *Chasing Catullus*, I found the personal (or the personalized) could intervene even when one might not expect it [...] The final poems in *The Word for Sorrow* return to the more personal, family history of the earlier collection, uncovered, often from chance conversations, as I worked on the book. (Balmer 2013: 225)

The Paths of Survival, the first – and also the lengthier – volume published in 2017, is a sustained meditation on the passages and rediscoveries of *Myrmidons*, the fabled lost play by Aeschylus; it tells of its inhabitations of consciousness across time, languages and geographical space. This sense is brought home from the very title of the 94-page book, which exists itself as proof of the power exercised by a few fragments in a papyrus manuscript on our imagination: millennia later in the case of Balmer and, as her dramatic monologues collectively argue, *in all the centuries in between*. These are attributed to several actors/categories (we come across 'Excavators', 'Editors', 'Translators', 'Anthologists', 'Annotators', 'Copyists' among the titles given to fifteen different sections, containing between one and five poems each) as they come into varied contact with the *Myrmidons*. The play's presence and disappearances are kaleidoscopically observed, from a witnessing of the fragments in The Sackler Library in Oxford in the present day, to the perils of war threatening them in Baghdad, in Florence or Constantinople, to stories of patronage, censorship or salvaging of the text that gradually take us, in reverse chronological sequence, all the way to Aristophanes' parodying Aeschylus in *Assemblywomen* (see 'Thread', Balmer 2017a: 68-9) and finally, to the dramatist himself; composing in Gela, Sicily in 456 BCE, reflecting on his own experiences from the battle of Marathon which drive his reworking of the story of Achilles and Patroclus from Homer ('Aeschylus' Revision', ibid.: 72-7).

The Paths of Survival is, then, from the very start, about desired rewritings *in the original itself*, about recontextualisation as part of the story of literature. Balmer's elaborate structure parades the various ways in which authors and readers share ownership of texts. Poignantly placed at the very end, the English translation of the surviving text of *Myrmidons*, barely three-and-a-half pages long, is annotated by Balmer on facing pages – in the penultimate of her notes (on Achilles' relating the fable of an eagle who dies saying 'The weapons by which we are vanquished / Come not from others but our own wings', ibid.: 84), we simultaneously encounter explication from a classicist *and* the onset of creative work; proof, also, of how often the core narratives of poems included in preceding pages coincide with settings, and travels of, translation:

> These lines are quoted in many works over the ages including scientific and medical tracts, many of which survived after being translated into Arabic in Syria or the libraries of Baghdad. These then came back to western Europe via the Moors of southern Spain, where scholars translated them from Arabic into Latin. (ibid.: 85)

In fact, the ambitious canvas in *The Paths of Survival* is consumed by all acts, gradations in between translation and original. For the ways it suggests the philologist within the poet, her thematising occasions from literary history, it is perhaps worth quoting one of the shorter poems in its entirety:

'EROTIC TALES'
   (Lucian, Samosata, Syria, 200)

I'd thought of myself as the new Homer.

But readers, I soon learnt, prefer horror,
sci-fi. My *Erotic Tales* pay the bills,
bring in the hard cash, the boys and/or girls.
Even Aeschylus, known for his weighty verse,
dipped his nib in the ambidextrous:
such sacred communion between the thighs
sighed his Achilles over pert backside
to top my list of things bi-curious.

> And who's to say I'm not as lyrical?
> Across the empire, at any scribe's stall,
> my 'lightweight' prose is still copied ten times
> more than dull, turgid tragedies. Is this
> a talent wasted? Or career waylaid?
> Weighty or not, they'll remember my lines
> when Aeschylus' plays have long decayed.
> (ibid.: 50)

Beyond the connections established in this monologue between psychologies of writing and the behaviour of readers – both changing little, arguably, since Lucian's day – there is also noticeable echoing of Cavafy. The 'poet-historian' from Alexandria provides a register, if not a model, for many of the voices we hear across *The Paths of Survival*. He is in fact variously situated in several of Balmer's poems, as we shall see later in chapter 4.

In *Letting Go* (2017b; subtitled 'Thirty Mourning Sonnets and two poems'), we move back from textual to personal history, the poems here written following the sudden death of Balmer's mother. Despite the absence of titled sections, the processing of ancient sources towards enabling expression of grief is reminiscent of *Chasing Catullus*. Similarities also include a largely chronological iteration of events, from the opening 'Lost' ('…We'd just spoken – / I heard her laughing, hanging up the phone – / but when next we gathered, friends, family, / one of us would be missing, tricked away', ibid.: 13, lines 5-8) to 'Let Go' (2017b: 41) that riffs also on the tale of lost Creusa, desperately sought by Aeneas, in Virgil's *Aeneid*. In between, there are poems indicating 'after' Virgil, Ovid, Thucydides, Homer, Hesiod, Livy, Ibycus and Plato. Several others, as Balmer reveals in her 'Sources and Notes' (ibid.: 46-8), relate less visibly to classical authors: they may carry embedded or title quotes from Heraclitus or, in the case of a 'Fairfield Church' (ibid: 28) that Balmer remembers visiting with her mother, lines 5-7 are extracted from Pausanias' *Description of Greece* (8.18.5). A few of the poems that follow ('Breaking the Pact', 'Market Overton', 'The Other Path', ibid: 29, 33 and 34 respectively) offer an intriguing alignment of English locales – Marazion or Rutland – with the Underworld. Allusions from the *Symposium* and *Theogony*, the *Aeneid* and *Georgics* where Orpheus and Aeneas descend into Hades suggest not only identification of places and parallels within the present experiences of a classically-trained reading mind, but also how such retellings of myth were already being exchanged between Greek and Roman authors.

The situating of ancient events, of fragments and aphorisms reported from a distant world into a psychogeography of Cornwall, becomes more pronounced towards the end of the book. There, a sonnet titled 'Seat' lifts its first half (ibid: 40, lines 1-8) from Homer (the *Odyssey*'s 9.21-8 where, as Balmer tells us, '[a]t the court of the Phaeacian king, Alcinous, Odysseus speaks of his longing for his homeland Ithaca', ibid.: 48); then, it positions Balmer, her mother and us as readers on a seat located 'on the coastal footpath between Marazion and Perranuthnoe'. Earlier in the book, it is the *Iliad* we are brought into, through the epic simile in 12.278-86 comparing 'the missiles of the Greeks raining down on a besieged Troy to snow falling across the land' (see Balmer 2017b: 46) and as the poet reflects on the aftermath of her mother's death:

SNOW
   after Homer

Out of nowhere, it flurries thick and fast,
early winter yet sharp as arrow shaft.
The wind calms. Grief is stilled. But it falls on
veiling the Forest hills, dark, distant Downs,
levelling fresh-ploughed farmland. By the church
it pales the priest's black coat as he clears paths
in vain, ghosts the bonnet of skidded hearse;
it dampens down crematorium furnace,
cuts off caterers, blocks would-be mourners.
Drifting further, across the south and west,
flakes catch on harbour walls like drying nets.
Now only the spray curved above Penzance
remains unblanched, grazed against those grey shores.
All else is wrapped in snow, stifled, silenced.
   (ibid.: 19)

The timeline gradually takes us from winter into 'Spring' (ibid.: 26), yet we simultaneously inhabit the present and the sixth century BCE as Balmer draws from Ibycus, *PMG* 286: a poet for whom 'the new beginnings of spring bring only fresh pain' (ibid.: 47).

Recourse to the 'Sources and Notes' is essential for the reader to experience in full the poet's intentions in verse like this. At the same time, it is exactly such deployments and 'creative exercising' of translation that confirm it as an essential aspect of literature. And within Balmer's work, these combinations and methods succeed in locating living tissue in the writings of the past.

3
Back to the Start: Alice Oswald and an 'Excavation' of the *Iliad*

Even though comparisons with Ted Hughes were present from early on, it is in the second part of Alice Oswald's career that certain points of contact become clearer. In her Hughes Memorial Lecture, given in 2005, she discusses *Moortown Diary* (1979) and argues that 'even more than Hughes's other collections [it] draws on Hughes's fascination with the theatre. He worked with theatres throughout his life, translating Lorca, Aeschylus, Sophocles, Euripides – *not as academic texts but as performable plays*', further adding: 'the particular, energetic, on the run feeling of his poems grew directly out of his own sense of Shakespeare's plays' (Oswald 2005; my emphasis). Proximities of poetic language and performance are there in her later work; particularly when she draws extensively from Homer, in *Memorial* (2011a) and in the long poem 'Tithonus' that forms the second part of *Falling Awake* (2016). Reviewing the first book, Chloe Stopa-Hunt (2012) locates the presence of Hughes in the treatment of classical material:

> [Oswald's] muscular nature poetry […] grounded in the Hughesian tradition, also follows Ted Hughes's free approach to classical adaptation. *Memorial* dispenses with the *Iliad*'s core narrative, re-framing the Trojan story as one composed of crowds and individuals, not of heroes: the poem sustains a balance between specificity and vastness, as though Oswald's poetics were equipped with a zoom lens.

In an essay (2011b) shortly after *Memorial*'s publication, Oswald argues that her removing of the main narrative was an attempt at drawing attention to the discontinuity of the text, its pauses 'unmistakably exposed'; so that now

> [s]tripped of its plot, the *Iliad* is a scattering of names and biographies of ordinary soldiers: men who trip over their shields,

lose their courage or miss their wives. In addition to these, there is a cast of anonymous people: the farmers, walkers, mothers, neighbours who inhabit its similes. *Memorial* is a collection of these anti-heroic stories, an Iliad of minor characters. Its divided structure, moving abruptly from the soldiers' world to the simile world without the distraction of a narrative, is my response to the *Iliad*'s porousness – an attempt to make space for what the earliest critics called its 'enargeia'.

The shade of Hughes is there, according to Stopa-Hunt, in a situating also of English scenes within this plan: 'The repeating epic similes which break up Oswald's biographies all draw upon a relatively familiar repertoire of images within English poetry, from hawks to deer, and the Hughesian note is strongest in these passages' (Stopa-Hunt ibid.).

As we have seen, between Hughes's 'literalistic' preferences in those prefatory notes for *Modern Poetry in Translation* and his elongation of material in 1999's *Alcestis*, the poet's practice is more compartmentalised, perhaps, than what could be described as 'free'. On the other hand, though not encountered everywhere, references to nature are noticeably heightened in Oswald's poem; she has also admitted a fascination with Hughes's interest in shamanism (see Oswald and Porter 2014). It is worth reminding ourselves of what Hughes saw as a key connection, one which returns us to Homer and the classics: '[T]he shaman's dream is the basis for the hero story […] it is the skeleton of thousands of folk tales and myths. And of many narrative poems, the *Odyssey*, the *Divine Comedy*, *Faust*, etc.' (Hughes 2006: 14-15).

Memorial is yet more proof of the core values of an epic persisting across time, as its content and characters are revoiced and reset. Like Christopher Logue (whose *War Music* at points casts a shadow, mostly in terms of abstracting and verbal urgency) and other poets and translators before, Oswald confirms the drawing power of the *Iliad* in the realisation, and rendering, of force; the metal of weapons and armour is inescapable. Her 'Homer poem' starts as an image of its title: an eight-page long list of capitalised names. Only then these names become surrounded by a simple structure of stanza and twice-told simile. It is a remarkably effective 'tagging' of lives and selves, brief glimpses of home and basic biographies of these warriors, which are earned at death's door, exactly when their story 'finishes here in darkness' (Oswald 2011a: 20). This principle can be seen in the following lines, alongside the poet's ability to convey a violent death happening to nearly everyone already:

> [...]
> OENOMAUS
> HELENUS
> ORESBIUS
> PERIPHAS
> And
>
> ACAMAS a massive man best fighter in Thrace
> Came over the choppy tides of the Hellespont
> And almost instantly took a blow on his helmet
> The spear pressed through to his skull
> Tipped with darkness
> It was Ajax who stopped him
>
> Like that slow-motion moment
> When a woman weighs the wool
> Her poor old spider hands
> Work all night spinning a living for her children
> And then she stops
> She soothes the scales to a standstill
>   (ibid.: 25-6)

The names are themselves essential to the composition; at the end of her *New Statesman* essay (2011b), Oswald arrives at the realisation that '[t]o translate them without putting on a voice seemed impossible. But when I peered beyond their descriptions, first believing in and then attending to the people themselves, I found myself caught up in something horribly powerful – something real.' The names should not be there, because '[o]ne of the rules of Greek lament poetry is that it mustn't mention the dead by name in case of invoking a ghost' (ibid.).

Beyond its existence on the page, there is also a remarkable audio reading of the poem (Oswald 2011c); based on this, we can imagine how haunting an experience awaited the audience across several performances around the book's launch. Oswald has frequently explained the experience as traumatic, in terms analogous to soldiers returning from a battlefield. Considerable preparation was involved as well:

> I have grids in my head; the tapping of my foot, my clenched hand, they are making visual grids. It's a safe prison that I have to keep myself in. I actually think of squares of rhythm. In a

sense I take no responsibility for what happens in a performance of *Memorial*. It is shocking because the *Iliad* is shocking because it is real. (Oswald and Porter 2014)

These reflections confirm the significance of this dimension sought within Oswald's poetics, and how performance may connect to the oral tradition and influences from Greek lament poetry, as another crucial element. There is a growing sense in which

I almost can't bear to put poems in books any more. But this is quite different from being an oral poet in the Homeric sense. The *Iliad* for example was composed in performance, not just performed orally with a text in the background. That's not something I could ever do but in fact I'm happy to be a hybrid, somewhere between the two traditions. (ibid.)

Her introductory note to *Memorial* (see 2011a: 1-2) again emphasises that Oswald's allegiance is not to the 'printed *Iliad*' but to the vital instability and energies of 'memorable speech'. Homer inhabits a preliterate culture – a fact also echoed by Eavan Boland in her Afterword for the American edition: 'For the reader of a later age, living in an era of fixed text, there is something bright and moving in this image of the *Iliad* as a river, not an inland sea, flowing in and out of song, performance, memory, elegy and human interaction' (Boland 2012: 89). Elsewhere, Oswald explains vividly her preferences of 'textual impermanence' and goes so far as to claim that 'what keeps the poems alive is a little forgetting. In Homer you get the sense that anything could happen because the poet might not remember' (qtd. in Armitstead 2016). This understanding was apparently fortified by an experience that acted as catalyst in turning the effort of translation into a poetry-making. When she started translating, Oswald kept missing the 'radiance' of Homer's similes, and in fact

[i]t was not until I lost my notebook and spent two months working without notes that I discovered how to realign myself so that not just the poem but the brightness beneath it was visible. When my notebook returned, I found that my whole method had changed. Instead of worrying through dictionaries looking for reasonable words, I would scribble the Greek on to a scrap of paper and then walk and wait – sometimes days – until the image underneath showed clear. Then I'd translate it. (2011b)

We might partly attribute to such events Oswald's growing interest in performance that depends on memory, her argument for 'how one might restore that kind of pressure to a modern poet – take away all the props and categories and let the poems fend for themselves. I think we'd all write much better under those conditions' (Oswald and Porter 2014).

This sort of discipline may also account for 'Tithonus'; that more recent, 35-page long foray into possibilities of performing poetry. Found in Homer, the myth of dawn's lover, the man who grows old but cannot die – an antithesis to the numerous dead of *Memorial* – is summarised alongside stage directions in Oswald's prefatory note:

> It is said that the dawn fell in love with Tithonus
> and asked Zeus to make him immortal, but forgot
> to ask that he should not grow old. Unable to die,
> he grew older and older until at last the dawn
> locked him in a room where he still sits babbling
> to himself and waiting night after night for her
> appearance.
>   What you are about to hear is the sound
> of Tithonus meeting the dawn at midsummer.
> His voice starts at 4.17, when the sun is six degrees
> below the horizon, and stops 46 minutes later, at
> sunrise. The performance will begin in darkness.
>   (Oswald 2016: 46)

– Oswald then proceeds to retell the myth in clusters of poetic lines separated often by swathes of blank space, with vertical dots and dashes seemingly reminding us (and the poet) of duration and rhythm, as Oswald's piece experiments with spacing and typography. (Most dramatically, this is seen in the way the final words in the poem's last page – separately titled, 'So he goes on' – gradually fade into white.) The opening statement above already indicates a listening experience, but this was further enhanced by Griselda Sanderson's playing of a nyckelharpa, a sixteen-string Swedish instrument, when the poem was performed at Southbank Centre on October 9, 2014, as part of the London Literature Festival.

'Tithonus' certainly fits within *Falling Awake* in terms of style, inclinations of typographical arrangement, as well as themes (including other references to figures from classical myth, notably Orpheus in

'Severed Head Floating Downriver', 2016: 6-10). At the same time, it turns into such a magnification of method and process already shaping the rest of the collection, that the poem could be viewed as a separate, companion volume to *Falling Awake*. It is the clearest vision so far of a poetry that may exist beyond our long-established, printed understanding of it. Introducing *Memorial* to its readers, Oswald already asks whether it is 'only oral poems that can carry the living powers of things, or might a literary poem (or a literary version of an oral poem) learn how to do it?' (2011b). It is a question that also serves to connect the problem of translation to that of expressing surrounding reality, in the written medium, after Homer: because there are

> real leaves still alive in the *Iliad*, real animals, real people, real light attending everything. Goethe put it like this: 'Ancient writers represent real existence, whereas we usually present its effects.' All the *Iliad* translations I know are full of silk leaves, dictionary leaves. Plenty of them tell the story well or give vivid equivalents of Greek phrases, but they don't translate the *Iliad*'s manifest reality. (ibid.)

'Tithonus' notably extends Oswald's systematic attempt, since *Memorial* especially, to return to an orality that would work in today's poetry by conjuring a theatrical situation. For Armitstead (2016), the poem can even be argued to resemble 'Beckett's "dramaticules", except that while *Footfalls* or *Breath* are conceived as play texts, this is presented as part of a book of poems'. Yet Oswald's interest in verbalising sound and space was there from the start; her earlier *Dart* (2002), a long poem about the river which included, and was extended by the speech of people around and interacting with it, features this note at the start:

> This poem is made from the language of people who live and work on the Dart. Over the past two years I've been recording conversations with people who know the river. I've used these records as life-models from which to sketch out a series of characters – linking their voices to a sound-map of the river, a songline from the source to the sea. There are indications in the margin where one voice changes into another. These do not refer to real people or even fixed fictions. All voices should be read as the river's mutterings.

The reader here is directed to unlock dimensions of poetry as a theatre of sound. Drangsholt (2016: 11) indeed argues that as tropes, '"sound map" and "source to the sea", are also evocative of Eliot's "auditory imagination", which relates the creative act to the capacity to listen'.

In this light, we can further understand Oswald's later insistence on modern equivalents for modes of composition, and impacts, of oral poetry. The 'absence of authority' she likes so much in Homer also effects those very real leaves and trees in an epic like the *Iliad*. They are so, because '[a]ccording to their position in the line and their case-ending, they will come accompanied by an adjective that fits the rhythm, *but it won't be the outcome of one poet's mind; it won't be marked by one poet's accent*' (2011b; my emphasis). And Oswald notes that this grammar consequently tends to be 'cumulative, like a cairn. Each clause is a separable unit' (ibid.). It is vital that she finds, for her *Iliad*, a correspondence to 'the cracked nature of [Homer's] syntax'.³ We further realise this earlier in her *New Statesman* essay, when she remembers returning, on Friday afternoons, from reading Homer with her teacher. A love for this poetry already shapes thought, memory, *syntax* – and crucially predisposes Oswald's as yet unwritten work:

> As a teenager, I couldn't get Homer's self-regulating patterns out of my head. When I walked out of that tiny classroom, along the streets to the station, then uphill through the woods, past the barking dog and the old buses, past the church, past Miss Waters hanging out her rectangular underwear, down the wet field home avoiding the ram, through the iron gate that always groaned when opened and into my mother's flower-governed garden, everything I saw seemed to be powered by its singleness. Everything stood next to something else but had its eyes turned away. All my poems have been translations of that pattern […] (Oswald 2011b)

Memorial, then, is a fuller elicitation of cognitions already there; it exists as a repatriation of this paratactic logic, turning it into an operating principle: it is there in the sheer accumulation of identities, the poet gathering human consciousness as it coincides with similes, inside the battlefield. Many of them in fact appear to walk the line between capable visual metaphor and the near-meaningless. The poet has already come to understand that similes are the 'inflorescence' of Homer's grammar, 'just

---

³ On these points, and about Oswald's associated 'dry-stone style' see also Thacker 2015: 44.

as loose and lateral in their connections' (ibid.). The repetition of similes amplifies, simultaneously, both futility and brutal force; suggests how these may exist before explanation, or narrative, or dramatic structure. The tonal effect remarkably conveys to readers *and/as listeners* the sense that 'the ruin and music of war are sensory, not logical' as Boland puts it towards the end of her Afterword (2012: 87 – echoing similar comments Carne-Ross made in discussing the Homeric world with Christopher Logue, several decades ago).

It is in this awareness that original, translation and poetry meet, and, moreover, in realising that literature's very origins lie in acts of remembrance. It is then no accident that Oswald subtitles her work 'an excavation'[4] – these are *real* bodies exhumed from millennia of text, and the poetry in this book is arrived at as we share, and receive, these lives. And translation, as part of this poetry, is poignantly divided: in reflecting perhaps the distinct sources contributing to a 'bipolar', as Oswald puts it, original poem (similes come from pastoral lyric, the warrior's biographies from lament poetry), she informs readers that 'my "biographies" are paraphrases, my similes are translations' (2011a: 2). She further elucidates a description of her 'irreverent' approach to translation thus: 'I work closely with the Greek, but instead of carrying the words over into English, *I use them as openings through which to see what Homer was looking at. I write through the Greek, not from it* – aiming for translucence, rather than translation' (ibid.; my emphasis).

'Excavation' or 'account', Oswald's and Logue's engagements with Homer are merely the last in a long series of re-animations, and necessary *intensifications*, of Homeric epic; both these versions are cognizant of the value of designing analogies of reception. In the case of Oswald, there is possibly more to come: following her performances of *Memorial* (that 'haunting thing to do') she has confessed in her interview for *The White Review* (Oswald and Porter 2014) that she started re-reading the *Odyssey* 'and I can't help beginning to think how one might translate it. Something very different from *Memorial*, certainly'. Pressed by the interviewer, she anticipates '[a] kind of ballad version, totally disloyal to the text. Because it's so much a poem about the sea, I'm interested in its dislocated way of working.' Later in the same exchange: 'I'm in mosaic mode now, translating, inventing. If I do tackle the Odyssey, it'll be much lighter and crazier than Memorial.'

---

[4] A year later, that subtitle interestingly, becomes 'a version of Homer's *Iliad*' in the American edition.

She adds, in spite of her own training, in implicit agreement with modernists like Pound and Logue before her: 'It'll infuriate classicists'.

Three

The Travelling Players

1
'Poems for Friends in Greece 1967-1971':
Richard Berengarten's Greek Experience

Collected in the pamphlet *The Return of Lazarus*,[1] a set of sixteen 'poems for friends in Greece 1967-1971' shows how the stay of an English poet of Jewish origins in Athens and Thebes radically influences themes and forms; certainly, in Berengarten's[2] output of that period, but also in the years since. Here, we witness an outsider's perspective coinciding with a desired naturalisation: the poet inhabits the realities of late-sixties' Greece (especially the repercussions of the military *coup d'état* of 1967), and voices aspects of a nation and its people:

> Freedom is not a birthright or a gift of gods
> but must be fought for again and again
> Four Easters ago I was free and did not know it
> I was young enough to think myself immortal
> never having tasted death in my wineglass
> I walked then on the olive covered hills
> and wallowed in the hazy ouzo evening
> and Rigas and Byron and Kolokotronis
> were textual problems for the classroom.
>   ('Eleftheria', 1971: 13)

---

[1] This includes *The Easter Rising 1967*, an earlier sequence protesting again the *coup d'état* that took place in Greece in April 21st 1967, soon after Berengarten's arrival in 1966. The ensuing dictatorial regime lasted until 1974. On the interesting story behind its first publication, as a poster glued into the January 1968 issue of *The London Magazine*, see Berengarten's insightful notes at the end of *For the Living: Longer Poems 1965-2000*, where he explains how the sequence was sent to England via a courier and how he presented himself as the poem's translator, assigning its authorship to a fictional young Greek poet who called himself 'Agnostos Nomolos' (Burns 2004: 157).

[2] Until 2008, the poet published his work as 'Richard Burns' before reclaiming his ancestral surname of Berengarten. Across this book, for volumes appearing before 2008 the reader will encounter 'Burns' within brackets (also, in the Bibliography at the end), but 'Berengarten' throughout the main text.

Greece, as a frame of reference, has affected Berengarten's poetry ever since, even if more subtly and sporadically. Yet these early poems more evidently double as a translation of the land and its people; most titles here are permeated with political-historical and socio-cultural references, with ventriloquisms of spoken language, considered analogies of tradition, and recollections of everyday experiences. And yet, even though the tone may be confessional in places, the poems are far from being autobiographical vignettes or straightforward impressions of landscape. The poet has always been more interested in meaning-making, and all too well perceives the imaginative transformations that define literary art, how it furthers originating experience, and how it must reach for a wider relevance.

In *The Return of Lazarus,* as well as in some poems on Greek themes that appear in Berengarten's first collection, *Double Flute* (1972a), the overriding sense is one of direct presence and identification. Poems such as 'Eleftheria', 'In his Ancestral Garden', 'Three Songs of Exile', 'The Funeral', 'Male Figure Playing a Double Flute' and 'Zeimbekiko' (the last two of which resurface in later collections) chronicle an intimate relationship that goes much deeper than mere idealisations of Hellenism or searches for antiquity. Rather, Berengarten's Greece, like Seamus Heaney's (and, as we shall see in following sections, Kelvin Corcoran's and Sebastian Barker's), is a living and lived space, where the ancient past remains contemporaneous, and the present is also one of encompassed histories: Byzantine, Ottoman, Vlach and Balkan inheritances also share the space and shape the people who inhabit it. Berengarten is enamoured with the resulting *Romiosyne*, that is, with the Greekness he encounters in all its multifaceted manifestations: the light always shaping the scenes around him; and the food, music and singing beside the quiet, weathered marble.

Taken together, these elements whisper a felt continuity that includes countless survivals, revolutions and resurrections – all of which, subsumed, also appear sometimes to connect to Berengarten's awareness of Judeity. Indeed, for the poet as an Englishman, Jew, Slav, Greek, or as an inheritor and bearer of each of these conditions, the dialogue between sensed identities and shared experience can prove productive, and uniquely so: 'Ode on the End of the Third Exile', the long, closing poem in *Learning to Talk* (Burns 1980: 75-9; see also *For the Living* 49-53), is an ambitious amalgam of eastern Mediterranean settings, both Italian and Hellenic, and of Jewish tradition and Greek myth. Here the first-person protagonist is pictured as a kind of travelling musician, a *jongleur* or *troubadour*, who embarks on a sea voyage. As the poem unfolds, there are allusions to the stories of Arion, Jonah and Dionysus (the protagonist indeed calls himself 'missionary for Dionysos'). More recently, in *The Blue Butterfly*, Berengarten's major sequence on a massacre of Serbs that took place at Kragujevac in October 1941 during the Nazi occupation of Yugoslavia, we come across translations of two songs from *Mauthausen* (1965) by the Greek poet Iakovos Kampanellis, who was himself deported to that concentration camp (see Berengarten 2011a: 45-6). Such moments of convergence – here found within what is perhaps the most potent synthesis of cultural elements, literary traditions and poetic forms of Berengarten's career, certainly until 2016's *Changing* – imply the wealth of recognitions assimilated in the course of the poet's wanderings. Embeddings of translation within a larger poetic whole, or across a body of work, make manifest the poet as a reader while contributing to literary design; and they are suggestive of a common, expressive core in both poetry and translation.

Such instances in Berengarten pronounce a mind that integrates disparities, and a poetics that strives to locate, beneath the drone of different languages, cultural perspectives and ethnic identities, the core values and psychological responses that should name – or remind us of – our collective self as humans. When asked to put in order his many 'identities', male, Jewish, English-speaker and so on, it is indeed no coincidence that Berengarten places 'human' first (Limburg 1999: 18). Elsewhere, the poet's self-description registers a conscious preference to identify himself as 'a European poet writing in English' (*Against Perfection*, 1999: inside back cover). From the beginning, a sensitivity to meaningful encounters of language, literature and culture as they realise or employ one another, comes fully to draw on Berengarten's varied experiences of 'living in translation' in Greece and former Yugoslavia (but also in Italy and the USA). It has already coincided with translations undertaken: notably, when it comes to Greece, of Antonis Samarakis's novel *Το Λάθος* (1965; translated together with Peter Mansfield as *The Flaw* (1969)). But further, this sensitivity, which may perhaps be likened to a kind of porosity, or semi-permeable receptivity, makes possible the empathy and inclusiveness that define Berengarten's poetry and are reflected in its formal variety. Furthermore, this quality not only helps us to understand his main themes of unity and justice, but also to contextualise his search for 'human constants', as well as his related search for universals in poetic expression (see esp. Berengarten 2013). This is not to mention a striking ability to understand and depict the diverse contents and manifold agitations of a modern consciousness, as he does to great effect in his book-length poem *The Manager* (2001).

Berengarten's early poetry is shaped by his Greek experience while also benefiting from the perspectives of the wider European tradition that he brings with him to these landscapes and seascapes. In turn, Greek elements find diverse entry points into his work, contributing to its multicultural reach, to its discoveries of what is shared in difference. As happens in 'Nada: Hope or Nothing' (Berengarten 2011a: 9), in which the poet's titular discovery of the different meanings of a homophonic word in two different languages (Serbo-Croatian and Spanish respectively) reaches an affirmation in a last line that is also a string of further translations of 'hope': '*Nada, Elpidha, Nadezhda, Esperanza, Hoffnung*' (the second is Greek). This tendency to see traditions share and compare is evident across the poet's activities, from early on, when he organised the first Cambridge Poetry Festival[3] in 1975. It was decidedly internationalist in its perspective, and as Berengarten recalls in one of my interviews with him, there was a Greek contingent, among them

> Kimon Friar, delivering a lecture in the debating chamber of the Cambridge Union, entitled 'The Use of Classical Myth by Modern Greek Poets', on April 21, 1975, months after the fall of the Junta and, coincidentally, on the eighth anniversary of the *coup d'état*. A forum on contemporary Greek poetry took place on Saturday April 19, with five participants: Kimon Friar, Katerina Anghelaki-Rooke, Nikos Stangos, Takis Sinopoulos and Nasos Vayenas. The Greek presence at the Cambridge Poetry Festival developed in successive years, culminating in the conference on Seferis in 1983. (Berengarten and Nikolaou 2017: 36)

Among numerous examples of the artists and poets of Hellas weaving their way through Berengarten's poems in references, echoes and intertextualities, there is the translated excerpt from Nikos Gatsos's *Amorgos* (1943) in the tenth section of *Avebury* (Burns 1972b; Burns 2004: 18-44), which ends with the lines (as translated by Sally Purcell) 'great dusky sea, so many pebbles round your neck / so many glinting jewels in your hair' (Berengarten ibid.: 28); and the (mis)quoting of George Seferis in the penultimate section of *The Manager*: 'So I've gone on trying till now. One

---

[3] For a fuller account of the Festival, its objectives and legacy see also Berengarten's article 'The Cambridge Poetry Festival: 35 years after' (2011b).

has to go on trying. No it's not the / past I'm talking about. I'm trying to talk about love') (Burns 2001: 153).

The influence of Yannis Ritsos can be felt in *The Return of Lazarus*; the rhythms of Odysseus Elytis can be heard in *Avebury*. The popular composers Mikis Theodorakis and Manos Hadjidakis are evident too: household names to Greeks because their music and lyrics are experienced as capturing and expressing this *Romiosyne*. Furthermore, folk songs that frame Greek life, in their marriages of words and melody, also echo through references to the *rebetika* tradition, especially to one of their major interpreters, Sotiria Bellou (see especially the already-mentioned 'Zeimbekiko', in Burns 1971: 9 and 1980: 41). Ancient thought (in the actual shape of Heraclitus, or suggested through Basilides of Alexandria who was both a Gnostic religious teacher of the 2nd century A.D. and a persona adopted by C. G. Jung in 1961's *Septem Sermones ad Mortuos*), figures from myth (especially Orpheus) and the remains of the past (the winged *Nike* of Samothrace, two *phalloi* on the island of Delos as well as Cycladic sculptures, all of which are set among the 'stones' of *Avebury*) all surface throughout Berengarten's oeuvre, finding their analogies and their references in the actual present and in the geography the poet inhabits or imagines. The occasional borrowing of Greek linguistic structures, the encountered traces of Greek poetic forms, the frequent transliterations of everyday items and actions: these complete the picture and serve to embed the reader in experiences that often coincide with their verbal construction.

More recently, the second of the 'Nine Codas' in *Book with No Back Cover* recounts a leisurely evening spent 'at the waterfront at Milina' (Burns 2003: 38-9) by what appears (from the names) to be an international group of tourists travelling to Greece's Pelion area. The poet is among them, his voice observing the people, eavesdropping on their dialogues and moods as he evokes the sense of the place. In line 9 of the poem, he writes: 'And now the sun, as the Greeks say, is *kinging* into sea haze' (ibid.: 38). The italicised word here is a literal translation of the verb *vasilévei*, as found in the exact Greek equivalent of the phrase 'the sun is setting'; thus verbal invention coincides with a translation that allows us to perceive, through Greek eyes, what has always been part of our experience.

2
In Memory of George Seferis / After T. S. Eliot

Equally significant is the dialogue between Berengarten and certain of his Greek contemporaries, if not more so – especially considering some recontextualisations of translation and formal experiment this dialogue leads to.

After meeting Nasos Vayenas in Cambridge in 1976, where the latter was completing a thesis on Seferis, Berengarten translated Βιογραφία (1978) into English, Vayenas's second collection. Crucially, the reading of each other's work has led to both translation *and* inspiration:

> Late one night, just after typing the final English version of *Biography*, I found myself doodling in my notebook and writing (not translating) what seemed like more 'parts' from *Biography*, or rather spin-offs from it. These fragments came out effortlessly and at speed. Then, as a *jeu d'esprit*, I had the idea of presenting Nasos with some 'new' sections of his own *Biography* – but pieces he hadn't written himself. I knew this would be in tune with his Borgesian sense of humour. Then I looked again at my doodles, and saw them in a new light. I realised that they didn't belong to *Biography*, that they were the first beginnings of something of my own. These were the first inklings, self-announcements of *The Manager*. (Berengarten and Limburg 2017: 46)

This long poem, eventually published in 2001, also notably coincides with discoveries and recognitions across two traditions, not least with respect to a longer line. The *verset* or 'verse paragraph', drawn initially from Vayenas (he himself adapts it from the Greek tradition), is a 'huge discovery':

> I only realised its full potential as I gradually worked at it, tracing its many precedents, partly through discussions with Nasos and partly through thinking more about other poetry and poets: for example, the fourteeners of early Elizabethan verse, Blake, Whitman, Ginsberg, Saint-John Perse, and Seferis. Since my student days, I'd been trying to develop a longer line for English, one that could be adaptable and flexible enough to bear the currents and stresses of contemporary speech-rhythms. Not just a *vers libre* line, but something more shaped, less loose, less flabby. When I asked Nasos where he thought Seferis had got *his*

long line from, he answered unhesitatingly, 'The Bible.' Then I realised what should have been obvious all along: that Blake and Whitman had both derived *their* own long lines from the King James Authorised Version, and Ginsberg from the Hebrew or Yiddish Bible. So, curiously, it turned out that the Bible, in various languages, was the key to my own long line too. A little later, in *Black Light*, which was dedicated to the memory of Seferis, I imitated his long lines. (ibid.: 47)

Further experimentation with this 'longer line', as Berengarten starts working on sections of *The Manager*, suggests that this form is extremely versatile and could indeed be a 'container for dramatic dialogue, straight narrative or description. It could equally well support specialist jargons, advertisements, business memoranda, fax messages, and so on. And it was capable of holding humour, parody, irony, sarcasm. In many ways, the flexibility of the verse-paragraph was the key to the realisation of my intention' (ibid.).

Similar explorations and exchanges are instigated on Vayenas's side, who includes a translation of Berengarten's 'Only the Common Miracle' (from the sequence mentioned above) within *Η Πτώση του Ιπτάμενου* (1989a; the Greek title translates that of Wallace Stevens's poem 'Flyer's Fall'. The volume poignantly articulates possibilities of poetic conversation: sixteen originals by Vayenas (several already echoing other poets) are interspersed with thirty-four translations: from Pound to Borges, H. D. to Marianne Moore, Calvino to Sandburg. Amalgamations are staged at such a scale that the reader witnesses acts of translation deservedly positioned within, and experienced as a vital part of, literary art. Key aspects of Vayenas's work until that point are further refracted, as versions and variations weave in and out of this assembly.

The origin of 'Only the Common Miracle' already names a shared elective affinity; at the same time, *Black Light: Poems in Memory of George Seferis* (1983/1995) is Berengarten's most sustained articulation of Greek cultural space. The twelve poems originally comprising the sequence involve the voice and gaze of Seferis, adding them to the thematic and stylistic preoccupations first encountered in *The Return of Lazarus*. The book begins with readings of and around the Greek poet that further direct our understanding: the first one of the two epigraphs comes from C. M. Bowra's 1957 study, *The Greek Experience*; the second is an epiphany that Seferis pens into his journal in June 1946 (there we read that 'behind the grey and golden weft of the Attic summer exists a *frightful black* [...]

we are all of us the playthings of this black'). The epiphany itself later metabolises in the long poem Κίχλη (1947, 'The Thrush'), a crowning moment in both Seferis's oeuvre and Greek literary modernism.

The English poet proceeds to explore these intimations about the nature of Greek light and grafts them to or associates them with his own:

> *Blood*, they insist through day, *Sperm. Sweat. Salt.*
> Crazy birds chirping, old crones cackling,
> village philosophers full of homely wisdom,
> bright eyed and red cheeked, children laughing,
> they purr, miaow, bark, they whinny, roar and howl:
> *Write, write,* they wail. *Sing with us,* they hum.
> *Do not forget your origin. The gold sun*, they shriek
> *is a black apple buried under the lake of darkness
> and we its pips, the black seeds of the sun...*
>
> Without them, no sky, no sea, no land, no light,
> no wisdom no madness no love no breath
> without them no song or poem
> No   they will never leave me
>   ('Cicadas (II)', 1995: 23-4; lines 28-36)

At the same time, examples like the above indicate intricacies of travel, poetry and life-writing. And even more so because it is *recollection* and dramatisation that coincide; the sequence was written in the summer of 1982, *after* Berengarten's return to England. Interviewed, he reflects on the project's gestation:

> [that summer] I wasn't able to go back to Volos, but experienced an intense longing to be there again. So that year, at home in Cambridge, I decided to allow myself to plunge headlong into 'Greek nostalgia' [...]. I set about re-reading all of Seferis's poems, as well as his post-war journal, in which he had made notes about the 'black light' while working on the poem 'Thrush' in 1946. That was when *Black Light* triggered. I conceived it from the start as a connected sequence, a self-cohering unity located in Greece and dedicated to Seferis, even though I wasn't entirely sure how many poems it would eventually hold. The fact that each poem in the sequence has an epigraph from Seferis reflects that they were all, in one way or another, responses to

his poems, as well as homage to him. Across a period of four or five weeks, I wrote most of the material in a kind of white heat or, rather, synaesthetic haze – immersed in Seferis, listening to Greek music, flooded by re-awakened sense impressions, and constantly working and reworking the poems [...] My inner images of Pelion were the freshest, and these resurfaced quickly. They account for much of the 'body' of *Black Light*. (Berengarten and Nikolaou 2014)

At several points Berengarten is strikingly inspired by internalisations of Greek language rhythms and poetic forms. There are constant efforts to relay idiomatic phrases in English; transliterations of place names, of everyday items and social ritual become a feature dramatising the dialogue between cultures and identities. From the two villanelles 'In Memory of George Seferis' which open and close the sequence (see Burns 1995: 7 and 25), to the prose poem of 'Shell' (ibid.: 22), formal variety synchronises with the metaphysical substrata lurking in the apparent warmth of Berengarten's chosen surroundings: Pelion, waterfronts in the sunset, tavernas, night covered hills, and the constant drone of cicadas, 'like waves of an inland sea' ('Cicadas (I)', ibid.: 13). The 'Notes and Acknowledgments' at the end (ibid.: 30-2) indeed confirm a wealth of Greek literary, cultural and critical absorptions (among them the chapter on the 'genealogy' of 'The Thrush' in Vayenas's by-then completed study of Seferis).

With so many markers of Greek language and culture transferred to and inhabiting the original, it is not surprising that an attempt at a translation becomes a return to bedrocks of expression, a reversal – meaningful in itself – of linguistic polarity. The interlinguistic movement here would illuminate the significances first conveyed in English; at the same time, it is in this kind of context that methods and processes of translation are furthered, and we may also observe it as *a literary site*. When Nasos Vayenas and Ilias Lagios eventually translated *Black Light* (the bilingual edition *Μαύρο Φως. Ποιήματα εις μνήμην Γιώργου Σεφέρη*, 2005), my review published a year later (Nikolaou 2006b: 168-71) discussed the sense in which this presented a sort of homecoming. Poems already drenched in what is Greek now face their translation – a translation that inevitably often coincides with 'un-translation: the fragments of Seferis in English revert to the originals, italicised transliterations of words like *kóre* or *tsípouro* and other cultural appropriations disappear into a "target language" now claiming its own fabric' (ibid.: 170). Other critics also discussed the peculiar effect of an English poem that feels more authentic in Greek translation, among them Maria Filippakopoulou, who proceeds to trace translating acts as part of the logic *of Black Light*'s original expression, further realised in how its Greek iterations will be received by readers:

> If lyrical language is to have any success in bringing about its undeadening effects, it needs a catalyst to rehearse the reality of loss, to *enact* self-alienation. In the translation by Lagios and Vayenas, the enterprise is played out in a format which obliges bilingual readers, at any rate, to look first into the face of the British poet turned towards the Greek poet laureate, before they can contemplate the work of the Greek translators and be struck by it manipulative energies. The multiple and zigzag reading is truly illuminating for it is responsible for the joy of recovering, partly at least, one's native tongue in the very midst of estrangement. (Filippakopoulou 2011: 209)

The poems that the two collaborators render into Greek are first and above all permeated by Seferis's voice. His poetry has already influenced their work enormously, just as it has influenced that of Berengarten. Here also, as often the case, the project of translation is a debt repaid. As anticipated, choices in the mode and format of publication simultaneously identify and serve to expand intertextualities in the source text; the translators' own poetic accents and habits can be traced, and the Seferis who is most readily recognised by Greek readers is also now irrevocably attached to Berengarten's *own* reading, and to his experiences. Indeed, I conclude in my 2006 review that Μαύρο Φως resembles a game of mirrors where 'originals conspire with translations toward scenes of recognition: the translating that attends the poetry is allowed to surface, translations reveal what they share with literary creation, the two poet-translators glimpse their own reflection in what [Berengarten] has made' (ibid.: 171). It is fitting that the Greek edition coincides with an additional prose-poem at the end of the sequence, as the English poet imagines an encounter with Seferis after death ('An Old Man in the Harbour', 2005: 58-63; facing a translation by Vayenas). This text reaches us as a kind of shared coda on an ongoing relationship – twenty years after the publication of the original English *Black Light*.

Vayenas has also written on the process behind the Greek translation, and his comments on dividing those thirteen poems between him and Lagios – despite their initial qualms that it ran contrary to the principle of stylistic unity in a poetic work – are worth quoting at length:

After all, the work we would be translating might itself be viewed as the result of a similar 'collaboration'. Indeed, it could be argued that the poems in 'Black Light' were not 'just' the work of Richard Berengarten, seeing that they expressed not only an English poet's lived, *personal* experience of the Greek light, but also his poetic, *literary* experience – though of course this was one that was no less uniquely 'lived'. In this case, the literary experience consisted precisely of Berengarten's readings of poems, diary-entries, lines and snippets of lines by Seferis – which explored exactly the same subject.

Viewed from this perspective, then, 'Black Light' could itself be rightly interpreted, or rather re-interpreted, as a *translation* of those poems and verses which had so clearly expressed Seferis' own sense of the Greek light, and of his experience of that mysterious quality which transformed this particular light into a symbol – first for Seferis and then for Berengarten – of light in general, of the centrality of light to human beings. [...W]e realised that 'Black Light' was interpretable as a *synthetic* poetic work: one that embedded the interplay of two voices, Berengarten's and Seferis'. [...] Yet while the text brings them together, it simultaneously leaves parts of each voice separate, unmerged – which enables each to 'refract' within the other.

In retrospect it is clear to me that this curious and singular 'inter-refraction' was another element that drew us both into this intertextual discourse. For, since we had both been brought up with (and within) the Seferian sense of the Greek light, and since we both felt an equally profound kinship with the 'black light' in Berengarten's poem, we decided that it was *appropriate* for us to add our voices to this translingual dialogue. [...] (Vayenas 2011: 178-9; trans. M. Eleftheriou)

Critical work and positions of translation often reflect on each other; for Marilyn Gaddis Rose, acts of literary translation normally 'bring us *into* the literary work in the usual sense of immersion and identification' (1997: 2; her emphasis). Boase-Beier and Holman (1999: 14) note that as a 'form of critical reading, and a concrete realisation of that reading, [translation] has much in common with the tradition of literary and biblical exegesis, commentary and exposition'. The literary translator, as Gregory Rabassa also reminds us, 'may be the one person who exists simultaneously in two different worlds: as he works he must be both critic and writer, writer and reader' (in Hoeksema 1978: 17). There are occasions, however when the workings of influence and of poetic intent, certain 'pre-existing conditions', arguably explode such relationships from the levels in which they generally occur. Beyond the obvious presence of Seferis, both Vayenas and Lagios come to meet Berengarten and his *Black Light* after long and already tangled histories of literary translational experiment. Some key instances should be briefly discussed in this section, not least because to some extent they prefigure the complex network of encounters and relationships between Seferis, Berengarten, Vayenas and Lagios described above.

In this sense, the textual status of «Η Αίθουσα», the poem which opens Vayenas's *Βιογραφία* is particularly interesting: As Morphia Malli describes in an essay on Vayenas's poetics (see Malli 2004, esp. 38-42; for a wide-ranging study see also Malli 2002), it is, in part, a version of Douglas Dunn's 1976 poem 'A Dream of Judgment' (see Dunn 2003: 11); several structures are retained from the English poem but there are poignant deviations that 'localise' it, transpose it to a different tradition. The figure of Johnson in the opening line ('Posterity, thy name is Samuel Johnson') is replaced by that of Dionysios Solomos (1798-1857; Greece's national poet) and the image of a 'fat diplomat' closing Vayenas's mouth 'with a hairy hand' in the penultimate line quite obviously turns our thought to Seferis. The poem that results from Dunn's poem (which is also *dedicated to him*) exists as a parallel comment on the Greek poetic canon, from a poet-critic whose own work also develops as a contemplation, critical and creative, of the poetry that may come after the modernist advances of this 'fat diplomat'. On the subject of influence, as it also relates to translation, what Vayenas puts forward in *Ποίηση και Μετάφραση* ('Poetry and Translation'; published the same year – 1989 – as *Η Πτώση του Ιπτάμενου*), is particularly illuminating:

> A meaningful theory of influence cannot be formulated if it is not supported by a meaningful theory of translation, because influence between two poets who write in different languages necessitates translation. In the last resort, the things that influence a poet are not lines in the original language, but those of the original transported into the poet's own language. No poet can take a poetic image from a foreign poet unless that image is put into words first, unless a rhythm of one's own language is instilled into it. Whether a poet will appropriate the lines of a foreign poem depends on how the lines of that poem sound within the fabric and rhythms of the poet's own language. This

does not mean that foreign influence necessitates a written translation. Each influence depends on there being a translation, whether this takes place on paper, or in the poet's mind.

(If the translation of poetry is an art, and if poetic influence requires translation, then such influence does not undermine originality. A foreign poet's text is raw material for a poet, just as is any other.) (my translation in Vayenas 2010a: 131-2)

Years earlier, in the study of Seferis's poetics (1979), key roles, imperatives and manifestations of translation were already being explored. Vayenas observes its workings in the bilingualism or multilingualism of Calvos, Solomos, and Cavafy, poets who are either in exile or constantly switching between cultures, seeing things from a distance, inhabiting contradictory points of view as different linguistic rhythms bear on their poetic sensibilities (see ibid.: 108). When it comes to Seferis, the focus is particularly on French and English influences: how the young Greek poet, who is writing his first verses in the vein of Laforgue and Verlaine, draws on Valéry's views on poetry; how he discovers a parallel life and elective affinity in T. S. Eliot; and how he proceeds to echo this influence, from unacknowledged, intertextualised appropriations of Eliot's lines and rhythms, to his more visible introduction of the Anglophone poet – and together with that, the entire modernist 'paradigm' – for Greek readers, through the translation of *The Waste Land* (as *Η Έρημη Χώρα*, 1936) or later *Murder in the Cathedral* (as *Φονικό στην Εκκλησιά*, 1954), a dramatic work.[4]

The relationship with Eliot, Vayenas suggests, is not unlike the one between Baudelaire and Poe, in which the former 'recognises' himself in the latter, and so feels he *has* to translate him (see Vayenas 1979: 181). In his later essay on Seferis as a translator of English poetry (1989b), Vayenas argues that

> [...] many believe his poetry would not be as we have it today, if Seferis had not happened to read Eliot. Indeed, it might be more accurate to say that his poetry would not be the same, *if Seferis had not translated Eliot. For one feels that it was exactly this process of translation which allowed Seferis to discover the depth of his affinity with the English poet.* (my translation and emphasis)

---

[4] For a detailed discussion of Seferis's approach in transplanting this uniquely configured theatrical work in the Greek context, see Letsios 2011: 16-26.

We should not be surprised to encounter Eliot in various modes and contexts in Vayenas's work, most poignantly, perhaps, in one of the sonnet-biographies in his next-to-last collection, Στη Νήσο των Μακάρων (2010b). The first quatrain of the English translation, published the same year in *The Perfect Order: Selected Poems 1974-2010* (ed. Richard Berengarten and myself) characteristically reads:

> April isn't the cruellest month. When you died
> in January, that was still harder to bear
> when even the lilacs bled
> and green was dressed in mourning everywhere.
> ('T. S. Eliot', 2010a: 117)

However, an earlier connection, and one that develops initially out of the language of literary criticism, results in a quite remarkable tale of collaborative re-imagining of intention and reception. In «Πάτροκλος Γιατράς, ή Οι Ελληνικές Μεταφράσεις της Έρημης Χώρας» (Vayenas 1976: 2-20; 'Patroclus Yiatras, or the Greek Translations of *The Waste Land*'), an entirely fictional personage 'discovers' Eliot and eventually becomes the poem's fourth translator into Greek.[5] This Borges-inspired story included in *Η Συντεχνία*, a slim book of three prose (para)texts, brilliantly transplants the dynamics of 'Pierre Menard, autor del Quijote' (1939) within the Greek literary tradition.

In this piece, which initially masquerades as a literary-critical essay, Vayenas's unnamed narrator-essayist informs us – on the basis of notes 'discovered after the translator's death' – that Yiatras believed that Eliot had failed fully to communicate the 'message' that had been entrusted to him by 'Poetry'. The reasons, in Yiatras's view, are said to have been religious as well as psychological; and he thus believes that it has fallen to him to put matters right. *But how?* Such an act of translation, as in Borges's fable, means one dilemma and paradox after another: for example, how in all conscience to exclude – from the process of transferring Eliot's poem into Greek – so many crucial historical events, both international and national: for example, Auschwitz, the Greek civil war, the atomic bomb, and Vietnam? Furthermore, how could Yiatras ignore publication history, namely the previous translations of the poem, which had already led to momentous changes within the Greek literary tradition?

---

[5] Patroclus Yiatras actually transmutes into a persona who is frequently encountered in Vayenas's work. For a detailed study of these (re)appearances beyond the 1976 story, see in particular, Pentzikis 2005.

As in the case of Menard, within Vayenas's literary and critical fantasy, we as readers experience no more than poignant glimpses of Yiatras's translation. But in 1984, Lagios, the same poet who would later collaborate with Vayenas in translating Berengarten's *Black Light* into Greek, arrives at a materialisation of this ghostly work. The beginning of his 'Notes' to *Η Έρημη Γη* (published 1995; English translation 2015 by Konstantina Georganta) – which are just as extensive as those of Eliot to the original *Waste Land* – clearly announce those quite fruitful machinations of reference:

> Nasos Vayenas' text 'Patroklos Yatras or The Greek translations of *The Waste Land*' («Πάτροκλος Γιατράς ή Οι ελληνικές μεταφράσεις της Έρημης Χώρας», 1976), which talks about a supposed – but no less possible – re-reading (or miscorrection?) of *The Waste Land*, was the starting point for writing this poem. I also have to refer to another historical work which influenced my generation significantly, namely *The Second Rebel Movement* (*Το Δεύτερο Αντάρτικο*). Let me add here that the narration takes place during one January day – apart from the fifth part which deals with the long time of night. In reality, the first four parts represent the dream of a working historical reality, while the fifth part, a dream's dream, is reality itself. Let me finish by saying that the poem's title refers to Solomos' 'The Destruction of Psara' where Glory
>
> > A crown upon her brow she wears –
> > Made of the scant and withered weeds
> > The desolate earth in silence bears.
> > (Lagios 2015: T19; [Solomos trans. E. M. Edmonds])

It is already evident from the above that Lagios is not interested in a re-translated poem, but rather, in one that is *repurposed*. Citing just the smallest section (IV) from his work, preceded by Eliot's original, allows us to gauge complex echoes and divergences, as the text is thoroughly metabolised, at the instigation of Vayenas's earlier 'translation' by the fictional character, Yiatras:

IV. DEATH BY WATER

Phlebas the Phoenician, a fortnight dead,
Forgot the cry of gulls, and the deep sea swell

And the profit and loss.
                A current under sea
Picked his bones in whispers. As he rose and fell
He passed the stages of his age and youth
Entering the whirlpool.
                Gentile or Jew
O you who turn the wheel and look to windward,
Consider Phlebas, who was once handsome and tall as you.
        (Eliot, *The Waste Land*, 1973: 486; lines 312-21)

IV. DEATH AND SEA

Arēs the Greek, for centuries dead,
Is remembered by the nightingale and the shadowy ravines
And the guns and clouds.
            A modest wind rising from the sea
Kissed his bones in song. Wed to the fight
He crucified his young life
To a place of mountains olive trees and sea.
                Comrade or countryman,
O you who turn the wheel and look to victory,
Consider Arēs, who was like you, and for you he died.
        (Lagios, *Desolate Land*, 2014: [T]14, lines 312-21)

Across this exercise in poetic reassignment, we witness an entire series of meaningful repetitions and/or differences, every small part of which is a holding point for Greek sociopolitical and literary history, now amplified through an emblematic poetic structure. Georganta argues that Eliot's long poem has inspired new possibilities in recording historical change through modes which allow the interplay of factual and fictional elements. And considering this sense, we are also reminded that

> Seferis was another poetic ancestor who had used a similar method in his long poem *Mythistorema* (1935) – where he had combined a certain mythology with an 'istoria', that is, in Greek, both 'history' and 'story' to express circumstances as independent from himself as the characters in a novel – and so it was an obvious choice for Lagios *to consider himself a descendant of them both when he chose to write a poem which would mimic their treatment of history and fictionality.* Vayenas' treatment of

a fictitious translator who supposedly died before completing a version of *The Waste Land* was the appropriate springboard for this venture. (Georganta 2015: 21; my emphasis)

As Alberto Manguel has indicated, there are some notable shifts between Cervantes and Borges: '[H]istory, writes Menard, is the mother of truth. "Menard," says Borges, "a contemporary of William James, defines history not as an investigation of reality but as its source. Historical truth, for him, is not what took place; it is what we believe took place"'(Manguel 2008: 113). Manguel continues,

> Borges's tongue-in-cheek distinction has a practical use. All reading is interpretation, every reading reveals and is dependent on the circumstances of its reader. And yet, if Cervantes's 'reading' of his text betrays the conventions of his time, among those conventions is the notion (less astonishing to Cervantes's readers than to Menard's) that history is what we judge to be history, that reality is dictated not by tangible facts but by those (in Coleridge's phrase) the reader's 'suspension of disbelief' renders real. (ibid.: 113-4)

This sense is borne out by rewarding interactions of voices in the Greek context, a continuation of the dialogue: recently, another published variation filled Lagios's metatextual model with socioeconomic commentary on Greece during the financial crisis; it was then printed alongside Vayenas's original account 'in the manner of Borges', Seferis's translation of *The Waste Land* (which Lagios follows very closely until the last part; see Georganta ibid.: 18), and of course Lagios's 1984 work. The texts are bookended by new critical essays (see Doxiadis 2017).

Beyond the large-scale dialogues that defined *Η Πτώση του Ιπτάμενου*, translations of various poets are found within most of Vayenas's collections. Stronger however, in his later career, is the presence of Gavin Ewart (1916-1995); indeed this presence coincides with the later half of *Η Πτώση του Ιπτάμενου, β΄* (1997), a smaller, sequel volume to the one published in 1989. Here, nine poems by Vayenas form the first part, followed by three poems by Ewart ('Climacteric', 'A Personal Footnote' and 'The Select Party'; see Ewart 1980: 131, 329 and 219-20 respectively), which now appear in Greek translation, two years after the English poet's death (see Vayenas 1997: 19-21). Tonal correspondences with Vayenas's originals that constitute the first pages of *Η Πτώση του Ιπτάμενου, β΄*

are further confirmed in Σκοτεινές Μπαλλάντες και Άλλα Ποιήματα (2001a). There, we encounter two poems («Έρωτος Αποτελέσματα» – also the title of the Ewart section in Η Πτώση του Ιπτάμενου, β΄ – and «Μπαλλάντα ενός Άδοξου Ποιητή για την Νέα Χιλιετία», see 2001a: 36-7 and 58-9) that are indicating «πάνω σε ένα ποίημα του Gavin Ewart» ('based on a poem by Gavin Ewart').[6] The second one was published three years earlier in the literary journal Ποιητική (1998: 198) under the title «Οικείες Αλήθειες» which immediately connects to that of the original ('Home Truths', in Ewart 1980: 356). The first two stanzas of both poems immediately suggest some key aspects of Ewart's work especially vis-à-vis his combination of the satirical and the erotic in a wry and witty tone; and paired with Vayenas's versions of the same lines, one quickly notices the economy and resourcefulness that characterise the latter's approach in rendering the poem in Greek (and these elements are arguably present even when a disclaimer such as a phrase like 'based on a poem by…' is absent):

> It isn't a very big cake,
> some of us won't get a slice,
> and that, make no mistake,
> can make us not very nice
> to one and all – or another
> poetical sister or brother.
> (Ewart, 'Poets', 1980: 312; lines 1-6)

> Δεν είναι πολύ μεγάλη η πίττα.
> Μερικοί δεν θα πάρουμε μπουκιά·
> πράγμα που μας βαραίνει σαν ήττα,
> που κάνει τον καθένα μας κακό ή κακιά.
> Μας τρώει μια μοχθηρία κρυφή
> γι' αυτούς που βρίσκονται στην κορυφή.
> («Μπαλλάντα ενός Άδοξου Ποιητή για τη Νέα Χιλιετία», 2001a: 58; lines 1-6)

> What the censorious wives,
> the ones who throw words like knives,

---

[6] In an interview with Manos Stefanidis in 2009, Vayenas mentions that in the few instances when this subtitle occurs, the process began as one of translation yet could not arrive at a result. It diverted instead towards more creative work, in such a way that a poem that may 'relate to' an originary text can also have an entirely autonomous identity of its own.

> have never understood
> is how it's the hen that pecks –
> not the hope of better sex –
> makes men leave home for good.
> (Ewart, 'Home Truths', 1980: 356; lines 1-6)

> Εκείνο που τα πικρόχολα ταίρια
> – αυτά που πετούν λέξεις σαν μαχαίρια –
> δεν μπορούν να κατανοήσουν
> είναι ότι η κότα που τσιμπά,
> κι όχι η ελπίδα για γλυκότερο χαλβά,
> κάνει τους άντρες να λακίσουν.
> («Έρωτος Αποτελέσματα», 2001a: 36; lines 1-6)

Such cutting social commentary often includes the 'business' of poetry itself, precisely by undertaking the perceptive examination of frivolous behaviour. Here, the terse yet deft manner belies a serious intelligence underneath that perhaps draws Vayenas towards Ewart's keen exploration and subversion of poetic devices. The English poet's themes may be equally suggested through use of limericks, the sonnet, or the haiku. Anthony Thwaite describes this tendency, and an example that develops from it, in his obituary for Ewart in *The Independent* (24 October, 1995):

> Ewart's vaguely roving eye was drawn to headlines, advertisements, linguistic nonsenses, even versions of literary history (as in his magnificent '2001: The Tennyson/Hardy Poem', in which he laughs at the pretensions of the poet, including himself, while actually achieving a consummate pastiche of both Tennyson and Hardy).

Ewart was very much influenced not only by Pound, Eliot and Auden, but also by contemporaries like Peter Porter, especially in *Londoners* (1964); and he was a master of the reconfiguration and appropriation of voices into new, mischievous formations. The junctures where the poet, as a reader of other poets, pays tribute while embarking on variations inspired by their work are frequent, even if sometimes oblique or reticent in disclosing where originating material is to be found.

And so it is often with Vayenas, as he converses with other poets. Acknowledged and visible instances of translating Ewart might only form a very small anthology, but the impact the British poet has had on Vayenas is remarkable. The above description of Ewart's poetics and overall outlook, together with the playfulness and irony enabled by formal discipline and concision, also apply to much of Vayenas's output, and more intensely so from the late 1990s onwards. The influence of Ewart is present too in the construction and role assigned to titles of poems, which very often reference poetic forms and include them in the text that follows (for instance, 'Sonnet: Afterwards', 'Sestina; The Literary Gathering' and 'A Ballad Re-Creation of a Fifties Incident at Barnes Bridge' (Ewart 2011: 86, 87-8 and 137 respectively)). If we consider this aspect alone, parallel comparison reveals striking similarities even before we come across conversions of thematic material or variations on it, for example in lines that seem to escape Ewart's poems but lodge themselves in those of Vayenas. A shifting but delicate balance between humour and despondency establishes an entire 'tonal attitude', which is encountered above all in the collection that the Greek poet puts out in 2001. This, together with Vayenas's critical work of that period, owes much to Ewart's influence, and is evident in internalisations of the latter's modes (see for example in Vayenas 2001b) where Vayenas argues that Greek poetry should move away from the excesses of free verse, and the ineptness that free verse has led to, advocating instead modes and models that are enriched again by formal disciplines and uses of rhyme. There are, it would seem, similarities of character and temperament between the two poets, common 'ways of seeing'.

Beyond the brief outline offered here, a longer study of these correspondences is essential in the future; for the dialogue is so extensive that it certainly merits singling out Ewart among Vayenas's key influences beyond Eliot. In the previous paragraphs, however, we have already begun to estimate how the British poet may have assisted the Greek: in furthering the latter's literary project, in amplifying particular qualities of voice, and, arguably, in his systematic attempt to steer aspects of poetic activity in Greece at the beginning of the new century.

3
Anthologies of Presence

Any discussion of poets travelling, and of the writing that results from it, necessarily starts with the admission of a wide range of outcomes. These may range from jotted-down itineraries, in which we struggle to identify a voice to which we have grown accustomed – as, for example, in Cavafy's diary from his first journey to Greece in the summer of 1901 – to those longer prose narratives that truly capture a consciousness and a sensibility in a certain place and period of time, in the specific context of a landscape, a people and their customs – for example, Octavio Paz's poignant impressions from his long stay in India as ambassador of Mexico. Yet another possible outcome is the kind of extended experimentation with poetic form that we have explored in preceding sections. In any of such resolutions, the foreign land quite often *rearranges* a poetic voice. In the case of Paz, the poems written about India or on Indian themes across a period of more than forty years (expertly edited by Eliot Weinberger in *A Tale of Two Gardens*, 1996) are so evocative that the poet himself more than once suggested that his travel writings devoted to this region were in fact 'footnotes to the poems'. Seferis, another diplomat, wrote extensively about his contact with Cypriot culture and historical events: Ημερολόγιο Καταστρώματος, γ' (*Logbook III*), his collection published in 1955 following his three visits to the island, is largely comprised of Cyprus-themed poems. These not only serve as a reminder of his experience there but also give a sense of completion to the essays and criticism that emerged from it.

What is more, these are often scenes of translation: we come across one such poignant episode in Peter Levi's memoir *The Hill of Kronos* (1980). The poet and critic (and Oxford Professor of Poetry between 1984 and 1989) arrived in Greece in 1963; he experienced the tumultuous years of the dictatorship and met several literary figures of the time. One of these was Nikos Gatsos, and Levi provided a preface for the bilingual edition of *Amorgos*, first published in 1998. Another was George Seferis, whom Levi last saw with a group of friends on a trip to Cape Sounion on 31st March 1971:

> We managed to get George to the top. He was triumphantly happy. [...T]he gorse was in full flower, and a lesser thorn, *tribolo*, lay here and there in dangerous cushions. I showed George Seferis how its natural shape, made a little bigger in bronze, was the ancient Greek defence against cavalry. One can see them to this day in museums. I asked him the Greek word for gorse. There was some discussion about that. George Pavlopoulos remembered a local name, *asphalaktos*, which had something to do with safety [...] Seferis was sure it was an ancient word, *aspalathos*, that had survived. That night, when Takis called late

> at his house, he had found his word in Plato. Soon afterwards he wrote ...*Epi Aspalathon, On gorse* (or *On thorns)*, his last, terrible poem. (Levi 1980: 174-5)

This poignant meeting of language and literary creation in the context of a Greece sensed across aeons is immediately followed by Levi's own translation of Seferis's final poem (ibid.: 71-2). Placed there, this somewhat paradoxically brings home, the ways in which a national self synchronises at various points with characters from myth, or redeploys forms from antiquity. It also clarifies how, for Greeks and non-Greeks alike, direct contact with this landscape may rapidly turn into intertextual dialogue with previous literature.

A profusion of examples of such richly layered experiences is to be found in *The Isles of Greece: A Collection of the Poetry of Place*, a small paperback edited by John Lucas (from travel book publisher Eland, 2010). Here, selections of Greek and English poets, from Sappho to Yannis Kondos, and from John Milton to David Constantine, offer a comprehensive picture, at key sociocultural junctures, both of outsiders looking in and of native authors visiting various parts of their own country. In addition, poems and extracts from poems are contextualised in thematic chapters that deal with aspects of island life, such as 'Sailing to Islands', 'Embarkation for Kytherea', 'Snapshots and Postcards', 'Island Love', '-Work' and '-Death'. Thus, specific locales, key historical events, staples of local cuisine, and discussions of everyday activities are continuously interrupted by poets' voices and cross-referenced against them, sometimes in the form of complete poems, and at others in long extracts or isolated lines. This extensive threading of literary quotations into the fabric of the text is achieved within the format of the pocket travel book, in such a way that the hybrid textual setting is made to cater to a dual readership: on the one hand, the knowing reader of poetry and on the other, the prospective traveller to Greece. The implication, of course, is that these two categories are considerably closer than we might think. From the earliest pages, John Lucas, who is also a poetry publisher – of Shoestring Press, – constantly introduces connections between poets and places. For example, he explains that Nikos Kavvadias was

> an habitué of Piraeus's waterfront bars, where, as he put it in one poem, 'shameless women catch the sailors', and in another, 'drugs are a slower way to die'. The bars are gone, the allure remains. After all, from here, as the different shipping lines and

ferries proclaim, you can sail to virtually all ports of the Aegean
[…] (Lucas 2010: 13)

Lucas's selections show the range of possibilities in recounting the Greek experience: from Menander to modernism, in both sonnet and free verse; from straightforward evocations of time and place to dense allusions to other poets, past literature and figures from myth. Both the scale and persistence of this 'poetry of place' helps us realise how often creating new literary utterance and seeking out previous ones belong to the epiphenomena of travel.

Especially when it comes to Greece, these landscapes are intensely written and rewritten; each writer already works inside a psycho-geographical palimpsest, a terrain that is shared. The fact that four of the poems included in *The Isles of Greece* are attributed to the editor ('One for Zeno', 'The Cemetery at Molivos', 'A Postcard from Andros' and 'Faith and Reason: An Aeginetan Dialogue', ibid.: 16, 33, 50-1 and 56 respectively), is in itself of interest, and it is worth citing 'The Cemetery at Molivos' in its entirety here. Connections made within the poem movingly reflect motifs that recur throughout the book:

> The cemetery at Molivos is on a shelf of land sloping to sea:
> you skirt the last, low farmhouse, its gnarled fig tree,
> follow a track round pink-hazed laurel bushes,
> past ambling, satyric goats, face heat that brushes
> dry, spikey grass to gold, and suddenly you're there,
> cypresses at each high white-walled corner
> jetting like wax-dark flame into blue air.
>
> On a still, sun-dazed morning we sauntered
> among those comforting tombs. Beyond, the sky
> was endless and so pure you said 'to lie
> here would be good, our bones safe from it all.'
> 'All?"
>   'The Bomb.'
>   I watched a caique haul
> anchor to put out on an unmarked sea,
> safe from clashing rocks or a god's fury,
> and thought what other furies had left their mark
> on this place of Arion, Sappho, Venetian, Turk …

> But that's all past – and why not dream that here
> our bones could settle down, that each new year
> the sun alone would burst across its sky,
> a goat's daft, randy bleat its one stark cry?

* * *

From this location, we may proceed to discuss some of the contemporary British poets who have travelled to Greece and been influenced, and even moved, by their discoveries there. In Kelvin Corcoran's writing, classical and modern co-existences are visible and concentrated: in five books published over the course of more than a decade, his poems about Greece eventually led to a collection, *For the Greek Spring* (2013), in which the Greek concerns and motifs that he had been exploring achieve full expression.

Faced with the scale of the poet's engagement with Greek subject matter, commentators position themselves accordingly: already on the back cover, Andy Brown, the editor a year later of *The Writing Occurs as Song: A Kelvin Corcoran Reader* (2014), asks us to

> [i]magine an ancient landscape hovering over the modern. Imagine a poetry of myth and political history overlaying and reinventing our own myths and songs; a poetry that speaks both backwards and forwards from the fulcrum of the present. Imagine a poetry that restores meaning to the group; in which mythology is local and alive and part of the everyday; in which story and song are the ways we understand ourselves.

Then, in his Introduction to the *Reader*, Brown details some key features: how Corcoran resists short, stand-alone poems despite his strong lyric tendencies, opting more often for 'arrangements' of poems in sections, where he characteristically 'uses temporal, spatial and contextual "jump cuts" to bring different time frames, locations and subjects, into close proximity' (Brown 2014: 12). In the same volume, when poet Peter Riley surveys 'Kelvin Corcoran and Greece' (74-89), he implies a shared set of influences and relationships.

Riley's own work relating to Greece merits a digression, especially the *Greek Passages* of 2009, which opens with a motto from Corcoran. This volume suggests even stronger connections between poetry and travel writing: four sections of prose poems ('ExoMáni 2002 (10 Preludes)',

'Argolid 2003', 'Argolid 2004', 'ExoMáni 2005 (10 Postludes)') feature dates prominently and remind us of journal entries. In examples like the following, the poetic form is tentative, left to be unfolded in the course of the act of reading:

> And such light I've never seen such light, all round us land and sea negotiating / over our blood, casting translucent banners across hard earth / Thin grey leaves fluttering, thunder in the hills, a new / wind across the harbour, the small boat setting out // The old women knitting in the alcove, keeping an eye on the mating rituals, threading the world into their harmony / The world watches, the small boat moving out across the wind / prow set for the world's end / for a year and a day. / Small chirruping cries, echoed along the coastal cliffs.
> (Riley 2009: 16)

In this way, days in the Peloponnese are abstracted into an overall structure where subtle comment on, say, the culture, or historical figures, inflects the poet's record of the surrounding landscape. The presentness of observation is obliquely haunted by movements from the past, lurking behind those everyday activities between 2002 and 2005.

In Corcoran's poetry, on the other hand, there is a higher concentration of detail and the dynamics between poetry and prose are exploited differently. A poem like 'Apokriatika' (2013: 92-4), describing a drive across the Peloponnese, opens with two paragraphs resembling part of a travel diary, documenting the customs witnessed:

Driving across to the Mani this February we broke the journey in Corinth. Slept the night in a stone cold room in the Hotel Shadow and ate at the taverna used by the villagers for a night out. We thought nothing of the children dressed in Pierrot costumes and Disney. Later I thought I saw a goat faced man outside the door in pitch darkness wearing a white veil, I thought his friend was wearing a Dolly Parton-style wig.

Next morning we drove on and saw big red and green kites on sale everywhere. Men standing and talking at the *kafeneio* were dressed in ball gowns and wigs. Well, village life we thought, you make your own entertainment. We found out the next day it was carnival – Apokriatika, the last weekend before Clean Monday of only fish and vegetables, but for now pre-lenten celebrations held sway. I remembered the carnival songs; cocks and cunts dancing around fruit trees, young boys being taken in hand by aunty at the mill and black straw faced devils chasing through the streets. (ibid.: 92)

Coming right after the title rather than, for example, in a note at the end, the prose here is an inextricable part of a literary design. The text then moves into a more obviously literary processing of this experience: to stanzas, rhythm and sense-making through form. Yet questions about the (re-)telling of memory arise regularly. In the central part, Corcoran even appears to return to 'another country' and to family histories (ibid.: 94): 'I know them only by her stories / and she's been dead more than twenty years, / they set out across Hardy's fields, / their rough old songs beating in the heart.'

A different balance is found in 'Byron's Karagiozis' (ibid.: 87-91) the poem which precedes 'Apokriatika'. Here, four quatrains are followed by 'Scenes' (numbered 1-4), imitating a theatrical idiom. Long descriptive lines that occasionally resemble stage directions combine with shorter, elliptical ones. As Corcoran explains in his notes (ibid.: 135), 'Byron was used as sexual bait for Ali Pasha, to win allegiance to the British cause in the conflict with Napoleon' and the poem was inspired by Ian Gilmour's book *The Making of the Poets: Byron and Shelley in Their Time* (2002). Other historical episodes instead turn to exercises in found poetry, as in 'The Objects Were Not Paid For or Got for a Fixed Price (Elgin)' (2013: 81; we also find inside brackets, in the right hand margin, names indicating quotes of Clarke, Douglas, Benizelos, Byron, Harrison, Smith). Poem-series, like those involving an invented 'Alexiares', embed cultural references spanning millennia. The meditative 'Alexiares in Exile' (ibid.: 52-7) mentions both Apollo and Xylouris. It also dramatises language, and a writerly self:

> Thalassa Mavri they sing, well they might – Greeks;
> I am in exile between textual variants,
> head down in darkness dancing out such poems
> would make the emperor of goats weep.

Corcoran's poems never romanticise the classical past or its actors; rather, through such 'jump cuts' or anachronisms, he examines complications and contradictions in the present: for instance, 'Epicurus Is My Neighbour' and 'News of Aristomenes' (ibid.: 20-3 and 95-111). Indeed, several commentators have noted differences in attitude between Corcoran and earlier British writers who tended to idealise Greece. Frances Leviston, reviewing *For the Greek Spring* in *The Guardian*, offers a contrast with Virginia Woolf's disappointment when she visited Greece in 1906: '[h]er expectations took no account of demotic Greek or the waves of occupation, immigration and exodus that had been changing Greece's cultural composition for centuries' (Leviston 2013). While Corcoran may be in conversation with Homer, he registers 'with equal care, the cultural pressures of modern Greek life', even though his title 'might lead us to expect more overtly political poems than we encounter' (ibid.) – especially considering popular protests against austerity measures in Greece in the year of publication. According to the same reviewer, the similarities with Seferis, especially uses of 'we' in 'Mythistorema', are also noticeable, since Corcoran's poems 'create a similarly choric space, in which tones and perspectives swim through one another, resisting readerly expectations' (ibid.).

Then there is also the figure of Pytheas, the ancient Greek explorer himself, who emerges in the last of the 'Three Monologues' (Corcoran 2013: 70-6): 'I watch the ships sail away and return, / captive in thought circumscribed by Strabo' (see 'Pytheas' ibid.: 74-6; lines 5-6). And shortly after that, comparisons with our present-day experience are suggested through the same voice:

> Has the world changed much at all? I doubt it.
> Are there still elites and prestige goods?
> Consider who wants you not to find out for yourself,
> add it up, exchange outside theogeny;
> for immediate and dangerous knowledge
> I swapped gifts with strangers and stepped ashore.
> (ibid.: 75; lines 25-30)

The poem proceeds from a reading of Cunliffe's book (in Corcoran's 'Notes', ibid.: 134-5, the poet cites it starkly as the source of inspiration), and attempts a lyrical intensification of experiences that were expansively assumed in prose.[7] Moment and mood are captured as Pytheas reminisc-

---

[7] It is worth registering here that Andy Brown, editor of the book of essays on Corcoran, produces 'The Tin Lodes' a few years later: his own sequence on Pytheas inspired by discussions with Corcoran and dedicated to him (see Brown 2016; prefaced by a note in which section IV of *The Waste Land* and Alice Oswald's *Dart* are identified among the influences).

es, dockside, in the lines that frame the main body of the poem: 'I wait in this room over the drink shop, / Winter wraps a cloak around the harbour' (ibid.: 76; lines 43-4). Pytheas' surprise and wonder at encounters in 'Pritanni' become more poignant contrasted with Corcoran's feelings of confusion and vulnerability in the preceding monologue ('The Ingliss Touriste Patient', ibid.: 72-4), which involves a health scare and visit to the hospital while travelling with his family in today's Greece.

These themes and juxtapositions continue beyond the 2013 selection. In *Sea Table* (2015), several stanzas develop as reflections while travelling: 'Blue hills of Argos like distant smoke / drift into Arcadia and the fertile valley; / white on white, after such blindness / we sat in the courtyard of a Greek spring' ('And Coming Back', 2015: 36; 3.2. – lines 1-4). From the very first pages, the poet constantly juggles time-frames and events. Occasionally he pauses, to revel in *being there*: 'Large as life Ithaka rolling under my feet, / I never thought I would get back here; / the sea never stops moving, the land now and then; / but here I am, I hold my nerve, I make it happen' (ibid.: 42; 4.4 – lines 1-4). It is a desire that extends to reach the imagined presence of fellow poets: 'Elizabeth Bishop' (ibid.: 64) '[…] leapt from the tender at Santos / danced across the snappy waves on sprightly toes / and swam the muddy tracks to Vigia' (lines 1-3). A few pages later, 'Sappho hit the water and rowed across the Aegean, / popped out like a cork at the pillars of Hercules; / at this distance each stroke a trochaic ripple / joined word to word on the manuscript of the sea' ('Sappho', ibid.: 70; lines 1-4).

But it is the final, titular part of a book comprised of larger forms and resolutely conjuring narrative, which returns wholly to Greece. In 'Sea Table' (ibid.: 93-119), we read of a sea voyage that starts in ancient times, with references that may strike us as familiar from Corcoran's previous book ('Change came across the sea / on a boat, men with different hair / their words on the water / their eyes sea-green asking', ibid.: 95; 1 – lines 25-8). After that, names and locations ('Gemistos/Plethon', 'Mystras', 'Monastiraki') move us from antiquity to the Byzantine era, through 'the Ottoman tide', with the poet's voice constantly interjecting ('I learned their language letter by letter / reading the names of their boats; / Captain Adonis, Maria Sunday, Lifeboat: / the sea's glossary made me its drudge', ibid.: 104; 2 – lines 61-4). We course through a story of sea trade and seafaring that arrives at the present day, when '[w]ords rise like birds driven off shore / scattered over the dark economy rolling in, / a country pirated, an evident blue removed', ibid.: 109; 3 – lines 8-10). And it is there when the archaic past and current experiences, language and language, link up more fully and inventively:

> The city bright gleaming stands and sinks,
> the smoke of riot clears and the poor are poorer still;
> no man a house of good stone not a painted paradise,
> τραπέζι τράπεζα try eating what's spread on that counter.
>
> Work out the big names, Xerxes, Caesar, Goldman Sachs;
> who can translate this lot for you, trace the etymology?
> But the music in the air at night is real classical, the song
> flowing backwards as it proceeds – and it's not made up.
>   (ibid.: 110; 4 – lines 13-20)

Several stanzas in this fourth section of 'Sea Table' feature sociopolitical comment and echoes of a troubled twentieth century, whilst connecting with Peloponnesian landscapes and the voice of another poet:

> Saidona is quiet, far off a man hammers his roof,
> the aconite, anemones and spilling daisies
> dance at the base of the memorial's white wall,
> an account, the many names, the lines by Ritsos;
> and the sky opens endlessly to the whole world.
>   (ibid.: 112; 4 – lines 70-4)

Most recently, in *Facing West* (2017), poems like 'Dionysus' attempt to relate ancient thought to modern consciousness, while 'Footnote to the Above' (2017: 28-32) checks on the ongoing financial crisis ('Eleanor at the taverna that night saying / – Of course the government has a plan B, / we run this business, even we have a plan B, / you see, they have a plan what to do, if if if' (ibid.: 30). *Facing West* concludes with 'Radio Archilochos' (ibid.: 57-80), a long sequence featuring various poetic forms first published in 2014. It weaves the voice of the poet from Paros – including some of the surviving fragments – with modern idiom, events and characters. Corcoran investigates the relevance of his dispositions and outlook in the present, the sequence ending in a call, 'Get up, get up Archilochos we need your bite; / will you bring us the news, say who benefits this time? / Archilochos has gone to the rushing night, the dark sea, / he hovers one moment in the light over Antiparos' (ibid.: 80; 5 – lines 121-4).

4
Collections of In-betweenness

As we have already seen with Richard Berengarten, allegiances to Greece's *modern* poets grow increasingly stronger. Results may include: book-length encounters, as in David Harsent's versions of Yannis Ritsos (*In Secret*, 2013; an overwhelmingly positive critical response to such projects affirms the need for more varied, subjective approaches complementing both 'translation proper' and/or a route of inclusion in anthologies or journals) – or even more constant echoes, like those of Odysseus Elytis in the work of Sebastian Barker.

In Barker's final collection of poems, *The Land of Gold* (2014) – he passed away very shortly after its publication – we are invited to trace his journey from the British Isles to the South of France, to its culmination in the Peloponnese and in the long sequence 'A Monastery of Light' (ibid.: 83-125; a further title indicates: 'The Sitochori Poems. A Village in the Mountains of the south-west Peloponnese'). Preceded by extracts from Odysseus Elytis's poems 'The Other Noah', 'The Autopsy' and 'The Light Tree', the author's note explains how '[i]n 1983, inspired by the modern Greek poets, I drove to Greece and bought a ruin in the mountains for £780'; he restores it painstakingly and '[t]his was to be my home from home for the next 30 years' (ibid.: 85). The sequence unfolding beyond this point is a superb example of 'poetry of place', to stay with the label offered in the Lucas anthology. Barker is able to link, in the space of a few lines, the immediacy of everyday observation, a romance of the foreign language around him, and an experience of landscape that involves history, a sensing of time:

> And in the village of Avlona, it is written on the road, *kalo taxidi*:
> have a good journey. The fields are strewn with stones known to
> the Mycenaeans, and the sun at noon is perpendicular, as it
> was to them.
> ('Sitochori', ibid.: 96; 12 – lines 7-10)

In Barker's case, the journey is also a spiritual one, the poet encountering his Christian faith along the way; but it is those extended stays in Sitochori that complete the metaphor of the poet's search for meaning. Both literature and autobiography are provoked by a simultaneity of foreignness and desired belonging. The intensity of being there is arguably responsible for the much longer lines in 'A Monastery of Light'; these hold more narrative content compared to the first part of the collection, where Barker will also offer brief glimpses of Greece, as in 'A Cocktail on Cos' (ibid.: 14), a vignette of island (night) life. There, 'Couples stroll across the streets, hand in hand, / Languorous arms draped over acquiescent shoulders' and 'Everywhere the sound of the unkillable *bouzouki* / Redeems back gardens, bars, hotels, even as a cockerel / Protests his ancient rites. The nearby concrete mixer / Is empty and pointed at the sky' (lines 3-4 and 13-6).

Evan Jones's 'Santorini' (in *Paralogues* 2012: 22-3) also offers a record of an island visit, one that incorporates the effort of remembering it justly. And there is that distance between experience and memory of which the poem is evidence:

> Our dream is to live here, in this moment, side by side
> and walking in silence always along the caldera,
> past busy cafés, expensive restaurants,
>
> hotels, blue-domed churches, whitewashed houses and stores,
> the light insisting along with the air that there
> is no way to continue, to travel deeper.
> (ibid.: 22; lines 16-21)

The very next line (and the rest of the poem) insists: 'But we find our way.'

An engagement with Greek themes, poets and tradition itself goes deep, and occurs throughout *Paralogues*, a title that takes us back to medieval Greek folk poems like 'The Song of the Dead Brother' (Jones's 'Note', 2012: 64, points out that 'παραλογές [ballads] [is] a genre word whose etymology links it to the illogical, the supernatural, things that are "beyond the logos", beyond the word of God') – inventively appropriated by Jones in 'Constantine and Arete: an autobiography' (ibid.: 39-62). This is an ambitious 24-part sequence that takes up half the volume and entangles the well-known material from tradition with the constant movements of early twenty-first century and elements from immigrant stories that include a poet like Jones (his father moved from the Greek city of Florina to Toronto in the 1950s). The fifth section (ibid.: 43) is a good example of how the poem is constituted:

> Her paternal great grandfather once mined
>   the coal seams of upstate Pennsylvania,
> a lefty and illegal migrant,
>   who unionized before deportation
> and screening by federal agencies
>   found him in Toronto. There he gathered
> his riches and left to build a rail-line
>   between Salonica and Florina,
> transporting hens along private iron tracks.
>   It's a story Arete doesn't know
> I know. And too far back for Constantine
>   who as a child longed for music, vinyl,
> like Myron's Marsyas, flute at his feet,
>   Arete in Athene's guise. Myron,
> a sculptor whose figures pointed forwards
>   so that anyone might follow to the past.
> I see them together, now, like statues,
>   Constantine and Arete, guarding
> the finished world. So it's not important
>   from where they've come or for what they're reaching.

There are other noteworthy inputs here, literary legacies that help Jones achieve this sort of synthesis: interviewed, he will confess that

> [Canadian poet] Richard Outram's *Benedict Abroad* is very important to a poem like 'Constantine and Arete'. I owe Outram an understanding of the long poem, of its possibilities, of voices, of a narrative progression which does not take over as it does in fiction. But then Outram likely learned that from Geoffrey Hill. And Hill perhaps from Eliot. (Jones and Campbell 2012)

The poems in the first half of the collection are no less remarkable for their exploration of concerns converging towards the event that is the long poem: there are several journeys and moments of transition (for instance, 'Letter to Sofia', and 'Bundesland Bavaria, between Deffingen and Denzingen', ibid.: 14-15 and 20 respectively) further supported by translation in 'Journey' (ibid.: 26; indicating 'after Miltos Sachtouris'[8]), and

---

[8] Among his responses to his *Maisonneuve* interview, there is a comment on how language, (poetic) identity and voices from the Greek tradition are sought in Canada, contemplated in translation: 'My parents tell me I could speak Greek as a child, but they

alternating with scenes like 'Justinian's Advisors Recall Him Prophesying' (ibid.: 25) that intensely bring to mind C. P. Cavafy (the Alexandrian himself makes an appearance in a British setting, as will be discussed in more detail in the next chapter).

Nowhere is Jones more interested in how art inspires other art than in 'Three Actaeons' (ibid.: 27-9), where an account of the myth is followed by a second poem inspired by Cy Twombly's painting 'Death of Actaeon' (1962/63), before we close on some lines 'after Raoul Schrott' (for the first publication of this English translation of the Austrian's 'Actaeon', alongside three more of his poems, see Schrott 2011). This manner of juxtaposing variations on the same theme, often through referencing of other art – painting in particular – can be found within individual poems (see, for example, 'Little Notes on Painting'; 'How I Became one of my Poems', ibid.: 10 and 30-1), and occurs also in Jones's first collection, *Nothing Fell Today but Rain* (2003). In *Paralogues* however, such references are more involved, and intertextuality works towards conscientiously naming positions in between literary and artistic traditions – paralleling perhaps the intricacy of the situation a Canadian poet of Greek origins finds himself in, especially since in 2004 he also became British-based.

The inclusion of prose elements or a tendency towards longer lines, verse-paragraphs and poetic sequences as found in Barker, Berengarten, Corcoran and Jones also speaks for situating material normally processed by memoirist or travel writer within the concerns and priorities of a poetic text. Others, like Vesna Goldsworthy, will instead compartmentalise and employ paratexts in allowing themselves space for autobiographical comment. Her *Angel of Salonika* (2011) is a particularly interesting endeavour in this respect. This first collection in English follows a trajectory that has seen the poet go from being a household name in her teenage years in her native Serbia to settling in Britain in the mid-1980s (she is now Professor of Creative Writing at the University of East Anglia, as well as the University of Exeter).

Though it starts in Greece, and a 'Summer on Pelion' (2011: 1-3), a place where '[t]he sea is implicit in everything', Goldsworthy's book

---

realised I couldn't communicate with other children so gave that up. I started translating in my twenties as part of my re-introduction to Greek. I figured it would help me build vocabulary, keep me in the language even if I wasn't using it every day. I'd read Cavafy, Elytis, Ritsos and Seferis, studying how those figures had become English-language poets via translation. I also knew there were others important to that grouping: Andreas Embiricos, Nikos Engonopoulos, Miltos Sachtouris. So I went at their poems – first with a friend, later with a dictionary. It was pure discovery for me, part of my education. I really wasn't thinking of publication at the time.' (Jones and Campbell 2012) evolves as an intriguing conflation of place-impressions. Even in this first poem where 'I am eighteen and a virgin, / I have a communist passport, / The summer on Pelion is unending' (ibid.: 2; lines 36-8), cities and geographies will very soon begin to contrast:

> We will travel the world
> But never again in such detail.
> I will meet you in London,
> Vienna, Cologne, Moscow and Bucharest.
> The Mediterranean will barely remember the Colonels,
> The exiles will return from their islands,
> The Wall will no longer divide Berlin,
> Yugoslavia will vanish and leave us unanchored.
> (ibid.: 3; lines 55-62)

In her eight-page afterword, Goldsworthy admits that '[m]y poetic imagination centres on that space between Rilke's Duino and Cavafy's Alexandria, and the Balkans remain at the heart of it' (2011: 48). In this sense, the significance of the title (also the last poem here[9]), certainly becomes clearer:

> As a city, Thessaloniki represents one of those complex and multi-layered places which are microcosms of the Balkans, with their rich and often contested history. Even my usage of a quaintly archaic name for it, Salonika (found in the English books which made me love its ancient melody), is not without its pitfalls. *Solun* (as I know it in my mother tongue) was both the springboard for a great campaign which decided Serbia's destiny in World War I, and the stage on which an intimate family event took place. (ibid.: 50)

Recognitions of shared history populate that titular poem (part VI, for instance, begins with a visit to the allied military cemetery at Zeytinlik) which poignantly culminates with the following two stanzas:

> Untouched himself by any thirst for luxury,
> Father spoke of Salonika
> In the First World War.
> We did not talk about the Second,

---

[9] In 2016, a Greek translation by Sakis Serefas appeared in a quarterly cultural journal published, aptly, in Thessaloniki.

> Nor dreamed that there was another one
> To come in our lifetime.
>
> I never questioned the reason for that silence.
> Long before I left for England I well understood
> That to be able to bear so much history
> One needs a circle of clear blue water
> Between yourself and it,
> A circle of clear blue water.
> ('The Angel of Salonika', ibid.: 45-6; VII –lines 9-20)

Elsewhere, the pain from the wars in Yugoslavia emerges even sharper: 'All your ancestors are dead or dying, / Their houses taken; / The wild vines grow / Inside the cisterns' ('Three Eighteen', ibid.: 26; IV – lines 8-14). The Afterword continues to provide insight into several poems and the mindset behind their composition: writing about that

> blazing summer on the Pelion peninsula thirty odd years ago, I vaguely recalled Seferis, climbing the slopes of Pelion while the sea climbed behind him 'like mercury in a thermometer.' I finally wrote a very different poem, but I had the same sense, as he had of Greece, that my homeland was following me, to 'wound me wherever I travel'. (ibid.: 52-3)

And so Seferis's well-worn line eventually becomes the epigraph to her *The Angel of Salonika*, implying that deliberate transposition; his Greece, her Serbia.

Such influences, and several others Goldsworthy that lists in the Afterword, of Russian and Serbian poets, 'provide a glittering palimpsest over which I have inscribed my imperfect English lines' (ibid.: 49). In fact, often arbitrary crossings of culture exist as an essential condition for the writing that emerges: after all, Goldsworthy becomes known in English through *Chernobyl Strawberries* (2005), a memoir where she first explores how she occupied different linguistic worlds. And an earlier study, *Inventing Ruritania: The Imperialism of the Imagination* (1998), in which Goldsworthy ably traces stereotypes (and ambiguities) in Western perceptions of the Balkans – the book includes extensive comment on British ideas about Greece – is also rooted in awareness of cultures that are fluid, always productively mingling, even through uneven power relations.

When it comes to poetic expression, Goldsworthy's Greece is a hub, a junction from which several lines leave for central Europe; other exiles are met or imagined along the way: 'The Birthday Concert' (2011: 35-6) is dedicated to Eva Hoffman and apparently joins her in suggesting that 'Poland will remain monochrome for years' (ibid.: 35). Goldsworthy writes in her Afterword that '[o]ne of the unexpected effects of emigration was a widening of my sense of a literary homeland' (ibid.: 52); another effect is encountered in how language tends to turn into metaphor and imagery by which an exiled self is understood, and dramatised. '[L]ike other writers who have had similar experiences of shifting cultures, of losing or rediscovering languages, she also stresses the physicality of language, the sounds and the gestures that accompany words' (Bassnett 2011: 76). Thus, the complex relationship between her land and Germany becomes now a dialogue between two lovers in the poem of the same title (ibid.: 37-9). Returning home the poet carries back with her

> [...] those long sentences of yours
> Which almost wound,
> Then retreat just before the full stop;
> Those untranslatable compound nouns
> Nailing more precisely the nature of our grief
> Than the palm of that familiar hand against the cross.
> ('Germany', ibid.: 38; IV – lines 4-9)

– the poem concluding also in the knowledge that 'In Luther's German as in English, / You are alone, *allein*, alone' (ibid.: 39; VI – lines 7-8). Or Goldsworthy will wonder – again in 'Three Eighteen' – 'Is it your language, / This gathering of salt crystals, / This clustering of consonants in your throat?' (ibid.: 24; I – lines 10-12). There is a duality implied in these lines, and it even includes what was once a mother tongue: as she discusses Goldsworthy's memoir, Bassnett quotes her on the constant negotiation between the Serbian of her early life and the English that is 'much more and much less than her mother tongue' (in Bassnett ibid.: 76); then, when Goldsworthy is working for the BBC World service, she comes to realise that she broadcasts 'in what itself must be becoming something quaintly archaic, the "RP" spoken by Belgrade's educated classes, the language which, in its own turn, both is and isn't my tongue' (ibid.).

In this sense, it is perhaps not entirely surprising that when her first novel, *Gorsky*, appeared in 2015, the English reader was faced with these concerns resonating in metatextual form. The prose here can be identified quickly as an appropriated, re-composed *Great Gatsby*, set in twenty-first century London instead of Jazz Age New York. The main character becomes a Russian arms-dealer who lives in Chelsea, and Fitzgerald's narrator Nick Carraway similarly turns into an immigrant named Nikola Kimovic. Settings and action all poignantly metabolise in reflecting the different forms, uses, strata and dramatic potential arising between literary translation and intercultural communication. It is a far-reaching rewriting; a novelistic experiment that perhaps could only be conceived and performed by an author with Goldsworthy's experiences.

In-betweenness similarly occupies Alice Kavounas's work. Born in New York to Greek parents who left for America (where she was educated at Vassar), Kavounas eventually moved to London, where she lived for ten years, then to Cornwall's Lizard Peninsula where she has made her home for nearly thirty years. Since the publication of her first collection, *The Invited* (1995), her poetry is very much preoccupied by place. While more recent work, as included at the end of *Abandoned Gardens: Selected and New Poems 1995-2016* (2017) celebrates the Cornish landscape (for example, in poems like '*Maen Eglos*, Lizard Peninsula', 2017: 110), it is a distant homeland and relayed memories of her parents' early life that impel much of her poetry. Sometimes, these will poignantly merge with her present life:

> What if, on a day in mid-September,
> I awoke as usual to this idyllic view –
> a crescent of a bay – but instead of Coverack
> it's my father's city, Smyrna, nineteen twenty-two,
> her harbour thick with battleships flying flags
> from the world's so-called fair-minded countries.
> ('Ornament of Asia', 2017: 56; lines 1-5)

Statements of (un-)belonging, weavings of memory and (personal) history are immediately traced in poem titles (the first three selected here from 2009's *Ornament of Asia* are: 'The Road to Ithaca', 'On Seeing the Statue of Liberty for the Second Time', 'Aivali' (2017: 49-52)); they are also prompted during frequent visits to Greece: 'Americanised, camouflaged in the dull plumage of drip dries, / you felt strong enough to untwist certain Athenian alleys. / But old intimacies have their underside; to go home / is to go barefoot over miles and miles of krokalia…' ('Abandoned Gardens', 2017: 19; lines 13-16). As in Berengarten's or Corcoran's poetry, phrasings in Greek or transliterations feature often; but given one's origin and family history, such almost talismanic uses of language are even more complexly felt here as part of the narrative, and drama of bicultural identity. 'Swallowing the Sea' (ibid.: 41) starts:

> 'Πέφτω. Ὅλο πέφτω.'
> *Falling? You keep falling, mother?* How weightless
> the verb is in Greek, twisting towards earth –
> 'a sere leaf' – it would be easier to regard you
> as a figure of speech. Instead, I worry
> at the rubbery spirals of the telephone cord
> like an old Greek thumbing his beads.

Deaths of parents are mulled over, returned to in fact across several poems; they are towering figures, and serve as links to the past: 'Head covered. Face, chest, legs – covered. But the makeshift shroud, / too short, exposed his ankles – bare, uncrossed, unmistakable. / And deep within him lay, I knew, his smoke-scoured lungs. The ocean / heaved him up; my drowned colossus, beached by the outgoing tide' ('Ocean', ibid.: 109, lines 17-20). In 'Foreign Mirrors' (ibid.: 131-2), the deceased prompts recognition over great distances – and a sense of responsibility coincides with customs in the old culture:

> Here she was, sent abroad to further her career –
> a concert pianist, like her mother. Even if she had the money,
> it would take four days to cross the Atlantic,
>
> another two, by ship or train to Athens. She'd miss the funeral.
> What should she do? Should she cover the mirrors
> the way they did in Athens whenever a relative died?
>   (ibid.: 131, lines 7-12)

Can and should this sort of ritual behaviour survive in the new world?: 'But this was New York. Could evil spirits, the devil, / reach this far, pass through glass to trap her mother's soul, / enter foreign mirrors? She has no one whose answer she could trust' (ibid.: lines 13-15). The dead mother is remembered alongside these worries in the rest of the poem. In fact, mourning is part of a verse that often memorialises scenes from this growing up between cultures but equally, the imagined or relayed experience of parents and relatives. It operates under the weight of their inheritance. We may conceive this writing as exilic in some respects, a consistent attempt to understand the effect of such absences, and returns, on the poetic imagination. And here, again, George Seferis is our guide in reading. Three stanzas from Rex Warner's translation of «Ο Γυρισμός του Ξενιτεμένου» ('The Return of the Exile') are printed right after the title page of *Abandoned Gardens*.

Endeavours of connecting with, and recording place are not only evidenced in the sheer number of poems in Kavounas's output bearing titles like 'Cutchogue, Long Island' (ibid.: 17) or 'Lunch in Ayvalik Harbour, Anatolia' (ibid.: 65-6), but also in her creating, with developer John Kennedy, a digital extension of such poetic inclinations. Essentially a location-based app, 'Words in Air: Poetry in Place' which entered Apple's iTunes store in 2014, began as Kavounas was teaching a postgraduate course:

> My students were welded to their mobiles as if life depended on it. This was the new screen. Personal. Private. Always with you. Perfect, I thought, for revealing places that spark great poems, bringing them into the palm of your hand. I named my idea *Words in Air* after the gripping correspondence between Elizabeth Bishop and Robert Lowell, both terrific poets of place. [The UK's] contained, varied landscape is what I decided I could map, with countless sources of inspiration for living contemporary poets, as well as Blake, Keats, Wordsworth, Coleridge, and of course T. S. Eliot, all of whom I'd studied at university – poets whose brilliance at evoking a sense of place drew me here. (Kavounas and Kennedy 2015)

The logic behind a project like this one is not dissimilar to that which inspired the small volume edited by John Lucas, discussed earlier. Away from a printed medium however, things become far more instantaneous and interactive: the more than 100 poems included in the app can be accessed from anywhere in the world, but the experience is much enhanced by presence, as the following excerpt from one of the early announcements of the project emphasises:

> Enjoy a poem instantly, on the very spot which sparked its creation. Discover new poems – and poets. Re-discover familiar places through a poem. See which poem was inspired by a place nearest to you, across the UK. Stand in the place where these poets stood, and gain a deeper insight into the poem, and

the place. Words in Air will pinpoint the place for you that sparked each poem. Visit, virtually and for real, to gain a deeper understanding of the creative process, through the revealing relationship between poetry and place. (The Hypatia Trust 2013)

The description at the iTunes store ('Category: Travel') further shares excitement about the possibilities of the idea and the platform:

> Simply tap 'Nearest Poem' to discover the poem closest to you. Not in the British Isles? Tap 'Surprise Me'. We'll take you somewhere new! Perhaps Suffolk, with Alan Jenkins? Norfolk, with George Szirtes? Housel Bay, Cornwall, with Penelope Shuttle? Whether you're going for a walk, on holiday, or an avid armchair traveller, you can access every poem, anytime, from anywhere. Over a thousand people in fifty-six countries are exploring the richness of our literary landscape.
>
> Enjoy over 100 contemporary and classic poems in Words in Air – an expanding anthology of award-winning work and fresh talent. Our 'About the Poet' feature helps to illuminate the poems. A website of the poet's choice takes you further into his or her world. (2016)

Projects like these can go far beyond a novelty factor, or a (very) welcome access to poetic language among the diversions consumed by a hyperconnected world. Given how many contemporary poets were encouraged to contribute poems to the app, beyond those inevitable key titles by Keats or Wordsworth, the hope is that such digital platforms can easily turn into an opportunities to quicken dialogue and reach distant readerships ('As a poet, it's very hard to get published in another country [...] It's a way of getting your poetry to a large number of countries'; Kavounas qtd. in *Vassar Info* 2014). At the same time, we can predict an increase in instances of such work as poets become aware that this sort of outlet exists.

We can even imagine a similar app, for Greece, reaching from classical times to the present; and to this in-betweenness we increasingly observe. It would certainly feature a contemporary poet like Fani Papageorgiou: Athenian-born, yet living in London and writing in English, her verse persistently positions the self in transit, in elsewheres. The two most recent books, *Not So Ill with You and Me* (2015) and *The Purloined Letter* (2017) refer repeatedly to travels in Greece; to cities already associated with poets who lived in them (Kostas Karyotakis remembered in Preveza; 'Travels Without You', 2015: 15-17) or to various neighbourhoods of the capital inducing memories of youth. The (literary) past is also recalled: on one page, we read of Thucydides and events of war in ancient Amphipolis, then on the facing page the white cliffs of Dover are poignantly mentioned before the modern poet asks, 'Why everything is foreshadowed in the *Iliad* / why do so many people die in the course of that book' (2017: 33; the greater part of the poem 'Seagulls', already an extensive meditation on the *Iliad* and its English translators). A chance visit to the Greek city of Alexandroupolis, near the borders with Turkey and Bulgaria (see 'The Delta', 2017: 35-62), triggers reflection on the fluidity of cultural identity. Inner conflict surfaces through observations of surrounding nature, (mis)interpretations of myth, and glimpses of the city's past merging with the poet's voice, as she passes through the region:

> Alexandroupolis was only a fishing village
> until the late 19th century.
> You're nine miles from river Evros.
> Memory is not the carcass of a whale
> on the ramp of an old port.
>   ('The Delta', ibid.: 41)

It is not surprising, then, that Papageorgiou's lines often exist as recognitions of how potently poetry and place connect: 'The brain is a mass of blood vessels. / Portals pop up in the oddest places – / forests, stones, pictures of boats', 2017: 67). Her efforts, like those of the instigators of Words in Air, like aspects of the verse of Berengarten, Barker, Corcoran, Goldsworthy, Jones, Riley and of so many others before them, would be compelled by this understanding: while prose accounts can certainly describe in detail the itineraries and contents of a journey, it is still a well-crafted poem that may truly transport us.

Four

The Shade of Cavafy

1
Early Encounters

Forster's perceptive account of the poet he met in Alexandria as an 'old man with a straw hat, standing absolutely motionless at a slight angle to the universe' is repeated often within critical approaches to Cavafy's work. Perhaps because it quickens our understanding: it works like lines of poetry. Conversely, the poem credited as being the first 'Cavafy-inspired' written outside of Greece, also functions as a review; a registration of literary developments: William Plomer's 'Sonnet to Cavafy: To the Greek Poet C. P. Cavafy on his Ποιήματα (1908-1914)', included in *The Fivefold Screen* (1932). Greek letters haunt the English title; and in the absence of book-length translations, Plomer is concerned with a lengthy selection in the original Greek, informing English readers of workings of reception within another literary system (for a thorough survey of Plomer's relationship with Greece and Cavafy – with whom he corresponded briefly – see Georganta 2010).

Since then, and especially after the expanded view those first book-length English translations by Mavrogordato (1951) and Dalven (1961) afford, the production of such work accelerated considerably. A few years after introducing the Dalven translations, Auden produced 'Rois Fainéants' (1968), a poem which embraces near-translation and simultaneously transposes Cavafy's 'Alexandrian Kings' to a different cultural milieu. Rather than a single occurrence, the poem stands as reconfirmation of the longer relationship already hinted at in the opening sentences of Auden's introduction to the Dalven edition (1961: xv, and cited at the end of my Prologue). Several other instances prefigure Auden's paratextual confession of the debt – for instance, the Ithaca-echoing 'Atlantis', written in 1941, balanced between homage and parody. There is variety in Auden's engagement with Cavafy, and it stretches across decades.

Lawrence Durrell, on the other hand, interestingly employs both poetry and prose, initially composing a poem titled 'Cavafy' in 1946 – it opens: 'I like to see so much the old man's loves / Egregious if you like and often shabby / Protruding from the ass's skin of verse, / for better or for worse, [...]' (see *Collected Poems, 1931-1974*, 1980: 38; includes also numerous poems thematically inspired by Cavafy). But he also features a character for the poet in his *Alexandria Quartet*, where several Cavafy poems also appear in the first and fourth books. 'The words of the old poet came into his mind, pressed down like the pedal of a piano, to boil and reverberate around the frail hope which the thought had raised from its dark sleep', we read in the first edition of *Justine* (1957: 181), followed immediately by eleven lines from 'The City'. The entire poem later appears alongside 'The God Abandons Antony' in Durrell's 'Workpoints' at the end of the volume, presaged thus:

> I copied and gave her the two translations from Cavafy which had pleased her though they were by no means literal. By now the Cavafy canon had been established by the fine thoughtful translations of Mavrogordato *and in a sense the poet has been freed for other poets to experiment with*; I have tried to transplant rather than translate – with what success I cannot say. (ibid.: 251-2; my emphasis)

Already, Durrell communicates an understanding of certain necessary steps when it comes to a poet's reception in another language. Further recasting of Cavafy originals may be found in three different passages of *Clea* (1960: 39, 40 and 140) where again 'the old poet of the city' is mentioned; asterisks then lead the reader to the 'Notes' (ibid.: 285-7) and to what Durrell calls 'free translations' of 'The Afternoon Sun', 'Far Away' and 'Che Fece... Il Gran Rifiuto'.[1]

These early, better-known encounters, scenes where the lines blur between appropriation, elective affinity and near-fictionalisation, certainly contributed to Cavafy's myth (on trajectories of this 'rise to fame' and the literary needs involved during this period, see also Dimirouli 2013). These scenes, however, are only the first in a long and expanding series. In 2000 we were allowed a better sense of the scale of poetic production that relates in diverse ways to Cavafy, in the selections included (translated into Greek) in Συνομιλώντας με τον Καβάφη – an anthology edited by Nasos Vayenas, a poet and critic discussed extensively in the previous chapter. It featured no less than 135 poems from 30 countries and 20 languages. For Vayenas,

---

[1] For detailed discussions of the presence of Cavafy in Durrell's work see also Katope (1969) and Pinchin (1977).

> no other poet of the twentieth century has directly inspired so many poets writing in other languages through his poetry [...] not because of some extraordinary event in his life, but almost exclusively because of his poetry. Furthermore, depictions of the man by his fellow poets invariably take the poetry itself as their point of departure. (2010a: 134-5; trans. John Davis)

What quality draws so many? Vayenas argues that

> [t]he unique dramatic and tragic irony in Cavafy is characterized by the systematic and highly refined depiction of the contradictions that exist between what *seems* and what *is*. This feature, which also serves to shape his verbal irony, is precisely what makes his language capable of eliciting poetic emotion, thereby rendering sensuous language superfluous. (ibid.: 135)

As a poet, Vayenas reflects such awareness of critical perspectives on Cavafy across several poems (see, in English translation, 'Clean Curtains' and 'Cavafy' in Vayenas 2010a: 54 and 115, and 'The Grammarian's Melancholy' in Nikolaou 2015: 25). He is certainly not the first Greek poet to do this, nor the only one to systematically consider how Cavafy's language operates. Seferis for instance, includes the following realisation in *On the Greek Style* (1966: 146):

> Very often in Cavafy's work, while the language itself is neutral and unemotional, the movement of the persons and the succession of the events involved is so closely packed, so airtight, one might almost say, that one has the impression that his poems *attract emotion by means of a vacuum*. The vacuum created by Cavafy is the element which differentiates his phrases from the mere prosaicness which the critics have fancied that they saw in his work. (trans. Rex Warner and Th. D. Frangopoulos)

It is from such recognitions that further poetry is created. Early critics, like Timos Malanos (not surprisingly, author of the first Greek Cavafy-inspired poem) wrote extensively on the poet's methods; the building and structuring of poems over long periods of time through a 'parasitic' imagination; a verse that depends less on a singular vision than on painstakingly combining and layering phrases or events (see 1981: 7-20).

He and others have provided detailed analyses of Cavafy's intense relationship with moments in the Hellenistic period in particular, and the significant influence the 12th Book of the *Palatine Anthology* had on the poet (Malanos 1957: 144 and 146ff; Ricks 2007: 149-69). In Daniel Mendelsohn's decision to entitle his Introduction to his translations in *The Collected Poems of C. P. Cavafy*, 'The Poet-Historian' (2009: xv-lix), we see this sense persisting to the present day, when the reach of Cavafy's verse has long gone global. From the start of this century alone, beginning with Theoharis C. Theoharis's *Before Time Could Change Them: The Collected Poems of Constantine P. Cavafy* in 2001, we count at least ten extensive translation projects up until the Martin McKinsey-edited, *Clearing the Ground: Poetry and Prose, 1902-1911* in 2015. (Auden again was among the first to pronounce on the translatability of the Greek originals – after comparing several English and French translations already in existence by then (see 1961: esp. xv-xvi).) A parallel proliferation of 'Cavafy-inspired' works strongly suggests a critical component becoming sublimated, diverted towards creative expression.

As the McKinsey volume at various points makes clear, there are inflections, conscious development, moments of self-doubt or self-confirmation taking place before the poet finds his readers, critics and translators. Nor should we undervalue a dialogue between traditions and languages already taking place in the poet's mind as the first originals take shape: Cavafy spent some of his childhood years in Liverpool and London in 1872-1877 and his very first poems, '[More Happy Thou, Performing Member]' (1877), 'Leaving Therapia' and 'Darkness and Shadows' (both 1882) were written in English.[2] Between 1884 and 1895 there were also exercises in the form of translated fragments of works by Shakespeare, Keats, Shelley, Tennyson (collected in Cavafy 2013). Even when his poetry was being written consistently in Greek, Cavafy was known to self-translate and privately circulate some of his poems in English before the task was systematically taken up by his brother John, whose translations – often still in association with the poet – appeared in English journals up to around 1920 (a volume containing the sixty-three translations was published in 2003; most of them can be accessed through the website of The Cavafy Archive).

Moving to Cavafy's actual reception in English, it is interesting to note that those earliest renderings by John Cavafy and George Valassopoulo

---

[2] The authorship, however, of the first and the third poem remains contentious to this day (see Ekdawi 1997: 223–30).

as prioritised in consultation often with Forster, or Cavafy himself (for instance, 'Darius', 'Alexandrian Kings') initially for purposes of inclusion in Forster's *Pharos and Pharillon* (1923), proceed to address figures in a historical period: suiting thematic norms in the target language, poetic writing that English readers would be familiar with. The three-way discussion between Forster, Valassopoulo and Cavafy about this undertaking, culminating notably on the occasion of 'Ithaca' appearing in T. S. Eliot's *Criterion* in 1924 – followed by 'For Ammones Who Died at the Age of 29 in 610' in 1928 – can be traced in 2009's *The Forster-Cavafy Letters: Friends at a Slight Angle* (edited by Peter Jeffreys, this volume helpfully includes the complete texts of the resulting published and unpublished translations). Today, many of these dynamics are very different – and of course, the field of translators and agents influencing Cavafy's reception is far more populated.

2
Contemporary Stances

An examination of the volume, and range, of Cavafy-inspired poetic production in Anglophone contexts certainly deserves far more extensive discussion. We may yet offer in this study some preliminary observations on an increase in situating Cavafy within the work of British poets in the new century. But certain unusual positions and backgrounds may be noted first: for instance, the Hellenist David Ricks (author also of several essays on Cavafy: see e.g. Ricks 1993, 2004 and 2007), publishes a poem titled 'Cavafy's Stationery' (2002: 147). In its psychogeographical transpositions, adoptions of tone and essential self-reflection involved in any dialogue between poets, it is worth quoting in its entirety:

CAVAFY'S STATIONERY

Accustomed as he was to holding things
Up to the light to see what others missed,
Did he ever peruse these watermarks?
Did Conqueror London make him muse on Empires
Once crescent, or Old Hickory evoke
A new world growing into history?
And did he start to dream of warriors

> Combing their hair, of their deep sense of duty
> – Not *so* unlike his to his craft and city –
> Each time his pencil marked the Spartan Bond?

Nearer the present, we encounter a book-length project inspired by Cavafy, in the shape of Louis de Bernières's *Imagining Alexandria* (2013). Primarily a novelist, de Bernières reflects in his Introduction that he is especially attached to the 'cameos of characters'; to the way this poetry is 'stuffed with narrative'. He immediately proceeds to clarify that

> in any case I have written under the influence of Cavafy, rather than in his manner. I do not follow his rhyme schemes, although I think that my metre is probably similar, and it is difficult to imitate his double game with katharevousa (a traditional, literary Greek) and demotic Greek, but there is some-thing about his perspective and tone of voice that has, I think, *infected me. When I come across an intriguing anecdote in Suetonius or Plutarch, I like to think that my little bursts of inspiration might be similar to those he experienced.* (2013: locs. 73-4; my emphasis)

Beyond reconfirming points of contact between poetry and prose, the fifty-five poems in *Imagining Alexandria* often draw on English locales and themes, and notably add heterosexual desire into the mix (see for example, 'Charity Function', 'Romance', 'For One Night Only', locs. 148-64, 319-35 and 474-87 respectively). The comments de Bernières makes overall are valuable in showing how the poetry of Cavafy particularly affects novelists (see Sotiropoulos 2015 for another recent example of this) as well as in further illuminating some inner workings: how impressions of – and a distance from – the originals, may relate, subtly agree or disagree with existing definitions and typology ('under the influence rather than in his manner').

In the case of Seamus Heaney – and here we may make one exception, given the unique position the poet occupied within the Anglophone poetic establishment[3] – the poet from Alexandria surfaces most clearly in *District and Circle* (2006) where a translation from the 'hidden poems' now includes the name of the poet himself ('Cavafy: The rest of I'll speak

---

[3] A recent study by Joanna Kruczkowska (2017) explores in considerable detail the productive relationship with Cavafy exhibited in the work of Irish poets, and in particular Heaney and Mahon. See also Fowler ('Plato, Seferis and Heaney: Poetry as Redress', 2014: 318-29).

to those below in Hades', ibid.: 73) and arguably forms part of a complex dialogue between the living and the dead across this collection, which also includes a poem titled 'George Seferis in the Underworld' (ibid.: 20-1).

Returning to Britain, and also to certain poets whose work has already been discussed earlier in this book, we contemplate, with Evan Jones, a 'Cavafy in Liverpool' (2012: 16) – '[…] in tweed and scarved, eyes closed / when the Mersey wind // calls his collar to his ear / on the strand near Albert Dock' (lines 3-6). This 'biography', John McAuliffe tells us, 'upends the relation between imagination and the actual, an act which also seems to describe Cavafy's habitual, everyday resort to Greek and Byzantine history in his lyrics' (McAuliffe 2012). It is not merely the sense of place, a dramatised dislocation that is also historical truth: Jones's poem culminates in the lines, 'One less wave, he thinks, one less, / and then the Persians can get through' (Jones ibid.: 16, lines 19-20). Here the young poet intimates themes to be written about years into the future, sharing with the contemporary poet, and the reader, a fictional moment of inspiration. In the poem and, indeed, the collection itself, 'Jones rejects sequence or any division between the present moment and the past, however conceived: as a result everything keeps happening at once. There's nothing orderly in Jones's (or Cavafy's) vision of the past as part of the present' (McAuliffe 2012). In an interview, Jones himself explains some of his intentions with respect to tensions between literary movements, the relationship of past and present (with the poet from Alexandria very likely falling among the 'favourite' poets):

> The twentieth century went back and forth so fast: there was Classicism and Futurism at the same time, Hardy and Apollinaire, Larkin and Benjamin Péret living only a channel away from each other. And there've been competing narratives at work as to which is more heroic – always to the detriment of the other. Some have even constructed narratives wherein the incompatible is made compatible, recognising the strengths and weaknesses of both (many of my favourite poets fall here). But allowing any one to exist without questioning it is a failure. Because in order to get to a version of the present, a version of the past has had to be eliminated. That's very much what *Paralogues* is about. I'm looking for the wealth in what has been decried as valueless. (Jones and Campbell 2012)

'Cavafy in Liverpool' is one among several Cavafy-inspired poems in *Paralogues* (others in this category would be 'Mr. Eugenides, the Smyrna Merchant', 'The Devoted Widow', and 'Justinian's Advisors Recall Him Prophesying' – Jones 2012: 12-13, 24, and 25 respectively). More recent work also channels Cavafy, such as 'Later Emperors', published in *PN Review* (Jones 2016a: 25-6) – and we see in parallel, several translations in journals: between 2014 and 2017, 'Anna Komnene' 'On Italian Shores', 'Apollonius of Tyana on Rhodes' and 'In the Port' appear in *Eborakon*, and 'Hidden' in *Poetry Ireland Review* ('In the Port' is notably followed by a very brief essay, linking migrant movement in Cavafy's time and in today's Europe especially in the wake of the war in Syria – see Jones 2016b). These translations emerge as part of Evan Jones's larger pursuit of the poet's reception, and as work continues on his editing *of The Cavafy Reader* (planned to appear in 2019), a volume that will also include a selection of prose texts.

Jones is not alone in showing this interest, and in fact literary periodicals are variously visited by Cavafy. In just one post-2000 number of *Modern Poetry in Translation*, we come across John Lucas's rendering of part of a 1984 sequence by Greek poet Andreas Angelakis that explores Cavafy's homosexual awakening ('Constantine in Constantinople', 2006: 32-6). The translation of this Cavafy-inspired work is immediately followed by two Cavafy poems, 'translated into Scots, via the French' in the same issue of *MPT* (Cavafy 2006: 37-9). Prefacing his work, translator John Manson informs readers that the French versions, as first published in *Le Semaine Egyptienne*, 25 April 1929, can be found reprinted below the ones in Scots. And such interesting connections are pursued often, by editors and translators alike.

In Josephine Balmer's work, translation has been more thoroughly subsumed inside a poetics of appropriation; Cavafy verses reappear as a consciousness transplanted in Britain:

> '78 NIGHTS
>   (after Cavafy)
>
> The room was dingy, always damp and dark – but cheap,
> hard to find, down the alley by the Courage pub.
> From the window all you could see was the brick walk
> by railway arch. But throughout that distilled summer,
> voices drifted up, wind-sent from the street below –

workmen, hacks, GLC clerks in C&A suits,
flushed on gassy beer and pressure-pump wine, the short
measure triumphs of pool and darts, trivial pursuits.

And there, on that sweated, sagging, second-hand bed,
we shared one body, one soul, till your lips became
my own, rose – no, the deep brown-red of vintage wine,
the stain that lingers long after the grass is drained,
so even now – years later – as I write alone
in my High Weald House, damp and dark and deep brown-red,
I'm drunk again on that same taste, same touch, same smell,
reeling once more at the red, red lies they could tell.
    (2004: 17)

Balmer's note (ibid.: 59) to this imitation included in *Chasing Catullus: Poems, Translations and Transgressions* makes the origin, and distances travelled, clear: 'A version of C. P. Cavafy's 1907 poem "One Night" which, like Cavafy himself, speaks Greek "with a slight British accent".' Despite the knowing use of 'slight', this is actually a rather forceful transposition, 'from Alexandria in the early 1900s to the late 1970s London of my student days' (Balmer 2013: 173-4). Not only personal memory but also the context for first presenting this piece may have contributed to its intensity. As further explained in *Piecing Together the Fragments* (ibid.), '"78 Nights' was written for BBC Radio/Arts Council Write Aloud scheme, which involved poetry practitioners in short literary radio features (along with explanatory commentary, the poem was then also published in the *Independent on Sunday* – see Balmer 1998).

In previously discussing Balmer, we have seen that such 'transgressions' may often exist as ventriloquisms accommodating moments of regret or loss. Such a case, and more complex textually than ''78 Nights', is presented by 'Cavafy's Things', originally published in 2013. It is a poem mourning the death of the poet's mother and is interestingly narrated by the plural 'we' of a family. Here, typical British town locales host recognisable words and translated fragments from Cavafy's well-known poem. For instance, in the middle part, an old table that is part of the family's history is rediscovered:

> [...]
> Now here it was in the newly-opened café
> (had it been an office for commercial affairs?
> Or maybe a solicitor's? No, the baker's…),
> lined round in pine, tarnished, second-hand;
> a resting-place for dust-caked builders
> slumped over strong tea, the full English,
> as dark and heady as funeral incense.
>
> *They must always have been around somewhere,
> those worn-out old things…*
> [...]
> (Balmer 2013b: 90; lines 9-17)

Slightly revised and re-titled as 'The Things We Leave Behind', Balmer recently positioned the poem at the very beginning of her 2017 book, *Letting Go*. As mentioned earlier in this study, this is an entire sequence of sonnets about the impact of this sudden death, where classical fragments are consistently recontextualised, meaningfully impacting on the present. Cavafy is the only modern poet referenced here, yet he is one consumed with analogies from the past and the workings of memory – something which further helps to collapse time and bring history and myth nearer our experience and Balmer's autobiography.

It is in *The Paths of Survival* (2017) however, that the dialogue with Cavafy's voice is perhaps most sustained. Balmer traces in reverse chronological order the surviving fragments of Aeschylus' *Myrmidons*, back to the tragedy's creation. Even though her book includes no direct references to Cavafy, parts of it are written to a large extent in his manner: they proceed from, and affirm, the value of the 'cameos of characters' de Bernières is in awe of. 'Sarpedon's Version' (ibid.: 64-5), to pick just one poem, while recognisably Balmer's work in terms of its prosody, is also propelled by an all too familiar sense of gazing at marginal actors in unforgiving historical scenes. It presents the reader with an argument, overall tone and conclusion that is very much indebted to Cavafy:

SARPEDON'S VERSION
   (*Athens, 336 BCE*)

When the call came from Athens for copyists,
scribes, I signed up at once; after two decades

still no one knew my name, I'd still not made it.
Even that tyrant Dionysus took first prize,
although his play had been greeted with hisses
and Diomedes, my boy, cried corruption –
we knew the charlatan had bribed the judges.
Diomedes' reward was to lose his tongue
and eyes, have the nose slashed from his bronzed face.

For all these sad years since I have guided him,
bathed him, gently walked beside at his own pace.
A few weeks ago I led him to a cliff;
the Sicilian sea below was a mirror
to hold the beauty of the world he had lost
and further out, in the dark, all its terror.
I whispered in his ear then let him step off,
the last three words we needed to hear or speak.
He could never have made the journey to Greece.

These days I transcribe Aeschylus word for word –
punishment, perhaps, for all the times we sneered,
sold his 'desk' to deluded despots, undeterred
by threat of retribution, we never once felt fear.
Lycurgus the archon guards my hunched lines,
ensuring each stroke of stylus is correct;
Athens must have control, literature defined,
the one, the only authoritative text.
And so I volunteered for the *Myrmidons* –

the fury of love lost, the blunt rage of hurt:
My love, my love, remember the nights we shared…
But even here I still dream, still have a plan,
I still believe there is time to make my mark.
I slip in lines, for myself, for Diomedes,
without shame now, our passion declared.
Now I am the hero, grief-struck Achilles –
yes, Achilles sighing to his Patroclus:
Soon I will follow you into darkness…

    Christopher Reid, whose *For and After* (2003) and work as editor of Christopher Logue were discussed earlier in this study, also features

Cavafy's voice in the list of 'C's that make up *The Curiosities* (2015). A title change will reflect Reid's overall plan ('Before Time Could Change Them' (1924) here becomes 'The Circumstances', 2015: 81), but there is also a notable shift with respect to typographical arrangement: each of the broken lines of the original (a key visual attribute in several of Cavafy's historical poems) unfolds in two lines in Reid's English. 'The Circumstances' thus interestingly doubles in length, though most other aspects remain close enough to 'Before Time Could Change Them'. In the same collection, 'The Cochineal', is arguably also inspired by Cavafy. Characteristically suggestive in its off-centre sketching of society gripped by (moral) crisis, it reminds us of poems like 'In a Famous Greek Colony, 200 B.C.' (1928) or even 'Finalities' (1911):

THE COCHINEAL

Now that the absolute
freshness of our brides
is less highly valued than it was before,
the makers and merchants
of cochineal, that costly substance,
of which every fluid ounce
represents the gore
of a thousand crushed insects,
have been the first and loudest
to denounce and deplore
the moral laxness of our times.
       (Reid ibid.: 38)

'Three Poems after Cavafy' are included in Don Paterson's *Landing Light* ('The Boat', 'One Night', 'The Bandaged Shoulder', 2003: 41-2); despite the designation 'after Cavafy', these are still essentially translations made by a poet. In Paterson's next collection, *Rain*, they are followed by 'The Bowl-Maker' (2009: 48), which resembles also a shift in approach, argues Evan Jones – as a researcher this time. In an unpublished paper (Jones 2011b), delivered at a conference on 'Poetry and Melancholia' at the University of Stirling in July 2011, he notes a more assured handling of material than in the *Landing Light* selections. Whereas these relied heavily on the Keeley and Sherrard translations, 'The Bowl-Maker' sees Paterson – like Reid after him – eliminating the original's hemistichs of six or seven syllables. Jones discusses also how Paterson reduces the poem's lines from twelve to ten, and even modifies the location slightly (the original 'Magnesia' becomes 'Lydia'). While this is enough to cancel out the connection to another poem by Cavafy (1915's 'The Battle of Magnesia'), Jones posits that the elegiac tone in Cavafy's original is retained, and carefully included as an earlier echo of the overall concern with loss across *Rain* – the translation here, acts also as 'evidence' for themes and experiences shared.

A year after the publication of *Rain*, David Harsent presents us with another such triptych in *Night*. His own 'Three Poems after Cavafy' include the 'Afternoon Sun', 'At the Tobacconist's Window' and 'The Art of Poetry' (2010: 57-9). Several comments recorded in an interview for the website *Podularity* (see Harsent and Miller n.d.) transmit the nature of such poetic dialogues, confirming key aspects of a practice that may arrive at just such a small, *embedded*, selection: Harsent has been 'reading and thinking' about these particular poems for a very long time; he admits that projects like these result from felt 'strong echoes', similarities in verse, overall, or 'at that point in time'. He is particularly interested in the 'process of filtration', the way something passes through the sensibility of one poet, then another when versioning; when the purpose is 'to produce a new English poem'. Asked by the interviewer, George Miller, for more details about his approach, Harsent responds that as he does not speak Greek, he asks friends and fellow poets – he mentions an Alice Kavounas among them – for literals initially; texts of absolutely 'no colour', as he puts it. With Cavafy of course, he is able to look into multiple translations, 'as exact as I can get' and then to 'triangulate'. Only very occasionally might Harsent 'glance at a looser translation' as he creates his own version.

Christopher Middleton's (1926-2015) engagement is longer – and more varied. There are some early appearances ('What Could You Have Made of It, Kavafis?', in *The Carleton Miscellany* 1963: 101) and indeed the Alexandrian is there almost from the start, as Middleton admits he is drawn to Lawrence Durrell's 'luminous heraldry, his Mediterranean glow' – and then 'soon enough, too, *the gravity, severity, the measuredness* of St.-John Perse, Eliot, Seferis, and Cavafy, attracted me powerfully. For all their rootedness in tradition, their poems have no trace of scripted or pre-scripted writing […]' (2005: 11; my emphasis). Cavafy's presence is recurrent across Middleton's hefty *Collected Later Poems* (2014), a representative selection indeed, published shortly before his death. Pieces like 'What the Hedgehog Said, A.D. 360' (ibid.: locs. 2017-23) rearrange

Cavafian references, unite them with Middleton's own observations of cultural life within history; others, like 'The Strategy of Apanea' (ibid.: locs. 1088-1102), more closely follow the economies of style, and proceed from a tone and perspective fully understood. At least two, 'Postcard from Alexandria, 1908' and 'The Typesetter's Visit to Cavafy' (ibid.: locs. 1894-904 and 5588-604 respectively) imagine the poet in close proximity. In the latter, the door is knocked at, yet never answered; the reader is kept company by the typesetter's ruminations while he waits outside:

> How you did wangle your way
> over chasms, step by step
> where no trails led but those
> you rediscovered, Sir, to kindle
> anew shocks of recognition that had knit
> their texts for ancient tragedies.
> (ibid.: locs. 5600-602; lines 28-33)

In many of the ways discussed in the previous part of this study, place remains important. Manchester-born John Ash, whose first collection was published in the late Seventies, increasingly involves Cavafy in his output after moving to Istanbul from New York in 1996, where he still lives and works as a university teacher. This is a poet already drawn to modes of historical anecdote, constructing scenes of encounter often set in Hellenistic as well as Byzantine periods. His interest is evident in much of his travel writing, most notably *A Byzantine Journey* (1995), but the thematic effect of relocating is striking: the fused cultures he experiences daily in Istanbul have energised, if not transformed, Ash's poetry over the past two decades – it is in this environment that he grows closer to Cavafy's registers of observation. *The Anatolikon* (2000) and *To the City* (2004) are populated with echoes of that familiar voice, as in 'The Names of Kings' or 'Displeasure of Ruins'; in *The Parthian Stations* (2007) these echoes continue as the ancient account of the route from Antioch to India connects with the poet's own autobiographical circumstances of relocation, and the antagonism of Parthia and Rome similarly echo Middle East conflicts in the present.

In the Wake of the Day (2010) announces a debt to Cavafy even more lucidly. There is clear movement from loaned style and imitation to extended translation. Ash includes twelve titles from Cavafy which literally and symbolically occupy a centre: in the middle part of his collection, this formation of poems[4] is also part of Ash's body of work and poetic intent. The number itself is predictive of a personal, subjective, *minimal* anthology. The name of the section, 'After Cavafy', is justified more by position than necessarily treatment of the originals, lodged as it is between the nineteen poems of 'The Women of Kars' (ibid.: 9-40) and a third and final part, 'The Bergamot Tree' (ibid.: 62-85) – both of which include lines and (place-)names referencing Cavafy (for example, in 'The Antiochiad', ibid.: 80-5). That is, even as Ash's approach is rather loose, concerned more with rhythms in English and an argument moving forward rather than keeping to the number and content of lines in the originals, he still does not digress from the originals quite enough for 'after' to signify a work of imitation or assimilation or deployment of Cavafy elements towards a new poetic whole.

There is, however, a compelling case to make that these chosen titles correspond to Ash's own concerns about the region and its past rulers, and the experience of exiles and immigrants. And there are exquisite exceptions to the poet's overall approach, ones that foster or amplify a sense of narrative, or even continue the one found within certain Cavafy poems. A couple of them are decidedly re-titled («Μέρες του 1909, '10, '11» becomes 'Without Memorial', ibid.: 44), and in two other cases we come across poems paired so that they are read and understood together: so this time, 'The Battle of Magnesia' (ibid.: 47-8) comprises 'A Maker of Mixing Bowls' – a poem written later, in 1921 – followed by the re-titled 'Battle of Magnesia' (as 'Sorrow of Macedon', and numbered '2'). Equally, 'The Triumph of John Kantakouzenos' (ibid.: 56-7) is broken into: '1. The Bishop's Assurances', which largely follows the narrative of Cavafy's 1924 original, while '2. Of Coloured Glass' is the title of a 1925 poem also featuring Kantakouzenos. In both cases, these are actions a poet-translator is far more able to take: drawing together material which would be separated by several pages in any (usually chronological) edition of Cavafy, though it observes the same character, or narratives around a particular historical event.

What is more, a furthering, or completion, of the story occurs in 'Fever of Kleitos' (Ash ibid.: 46-7). As can be seen below, the first part largely follows the progression in the original, in ways ably suggesting John Ash's priorities when it comes to translation:

---

[4] The titles as they appear between pages 44 and 60, are: 'Without Memorial', 'Fever of Kleitos', 'The Battle of Magnesia', 'Antiochus Epiphanes', 'The Gods in their Wisdom', 'In Osroene', 'Disillusionment of Demetrius Soter', 'The Triumph of John Kantakouzenos', 'Exiles', 'A Byzantine Nobleman Writing in Exile', 'In a Syrian Harbour'.

Η ΑΡΡΩΣΤΙΑ ΤΟΥ ΚΛΕΙΤΟΥ (1926)

Ο Κλείτος, ένα συμπαθητικό
παιδί, περίπου είκοσι τριώ ετών —
με αρίστην αγωγή, με σπάνια ελληνομάθεια —
είν' άρρωστος βαρειά. Τον ηύρε ο πυρετός
που φέτος θέρισε στην Αλεξάνδρεια.

Τον ηύρε ο πυρετός εξαντλημένο κιόλας ηθικώς
απ' τον καϋμό που ο εταίρος του, ένας νέος ηθοποιός,
έπαυσε να τον αγαπά και να τον θέλει.

Είν' άρρωστος βαρειά, και τρέμουν οι γονείς του.

Και μια γρηά υπηρέτρια που τον μεγάλωσε,
τρέμει κι' αυτή για την ζωή του Κλείτου.
Μες στην δεινήν ανησυχία της
στον νου της έρχεται ένα είδωλο
που λάτρευε μικρή, πριν μπει αυτού, υπηρέτρια,
σε σπίτι Χριστιανών επιφανών, και χριστιανέψει.
Παίρνει κρυφά κάτι πλακούντια, και κρασί, και μέλι.
Τα πάει στο είδωλο μπροστά. Όσα θυμάται μέλη
της ικεσίας ψάλλει· άκρες, μέσες. Η κουτή
δεν νοιώθει που τον μαύρον δαίμονα λίγο τον μέλει
αν γιάνει ή αν δεν γιάνει ένας Χριστιανός.

FEVER OF KLEITOS

I
Kleitos, a young man well-liked by all,
And some twenty-three years of age,
Son of a distinguished family, possessed
Of a refined knowledge of the Greek classics,
Has fallen desperately ill. The fever that ravaged
Alexandria this year has found him out –

Has found him already weakened by despair,
Knowing that the young actor he doted on
No longer desires him, no longer wants him around.

His condition is critical.
His terrified parents don't know where to turn.

An old maidservant, who helped raise him,
Also trembles with fear. In her agitation,
She suddenly recalls an idol she worshipped
As a child before she came as a servant
To this noble household of Christians,
And herself became a Christian. In secret,
She bakes votive breads, brings wine and honey,
And sets them before the idol. In no particular order,
She mumbles fragments of hymns and prayers,
Dimly remembered, not realising, poor fool,
That to her little black demon, whether a Christian
Lives or dies is a matter of complete indifference.

What follows (ibid.: 46-7) may perhaps remind the reader of a sort of inversion of attitudes described in a few Cavafy poems, for instance 'Myres: Alexandria A.D. 340' (1929) but is nowhere to be found in the canon. Rather, it is an original by Ash, written in the manner of Cavafy, appended to 'Kleitos' – an imagining of a poem that could have existed, and the other side of a story:

2
They say Kleitos asked for me on his deathbed.
I was touched, of course, but did not go.
Only a fool would have done so. The fever
That killed him was fiercely contagious,
And my love for him had died some months before.
Someone came along who excited me more.

True, the Gods can be cruel sometimes,
But how can I be blamed for that?

Nor did I attend the funeral,
He was a Christian after all,
And I cannot abide the religion, besides
His family might not have allowed it.
One thing I could do for him without risk,

> Without betraying my deepest convictions –
> Place flowers on his grave, jasmine and roses.

At the onset of those Cavafian (re-)appearances, ranging from relatively simple recontextualisation and embeddings of translation inside poetry collections, to more experimental approaches, lies a resolve to share a mind. In poems like 'Cavafy's Stationery' or 'Sarpedon's Version' we recall initial understandings whilst that familiar gaze is sensed to extend to other geographies and timeframes.

Meanwhile, we have come a long way since Mavrogordato's first book-length presentation of Cavafy in English, nearly seventy years ago; there is now a prismatic environment where the knowing, English-speaking reader may access a palimpsest of wordings and small shifts of emphasis. We note also that this Greek poetic voice has continued in another language through a remarkable inter- and paratextual operation; materialising and resonating in the cross-pollination of translational, critical and creative realms. Cavafy's status is reflected in those associations of actual translation and poems like Jones's 'Cavafy in Liverpool', Ash's addition to Kleitos' story, or the dialogues established in the work of new poets like Kim Moore (*The Art of Falling*, 2015). Indeed, such re-tellings of Cavafy, the rich results of what has become a code between poets, derive from the originals new and unexpected kinds of energy. In turn, they enhance our understanding of this verse and effect a visibility that also agitates new translations. And in many of the examples above we have our answer to Auden wondering in 1961, how it could be possible to be so thoroughly influenced by poetry in translation.

Afterword

Periplous

Towards the end of *Translation and the Poet's Life: The Ethics of Translating in English Culture, 1646-1726* (2008), Paul Davis takes note of John Gay's poem 'Mr Pope's Welcome from Greece' (1719), published on the occasion of the final volume of the translated *Iliad*. 'Bonfires do blaze & Bones and Cleavers ring / As at the coming of a mighty King' (lines 23-4), now that Pope returns home to Twickenham. Davis brings our attention also to the poet himself, describing the culmination of his efforts to William Broome in a letter in February of the same year: 'a conscientious discharge of all my debts and duties [...]'; and so, while Gay pictures Pope's Homeric voyage as a *translation imperii*, Pope exudes the 'weary relief of a storm-battered merchant' (Davis ibid.: 237). Underlying both letter and poem however, is 'the metaphor of translation as a sea voyage which launched scores of commendatory poems to the Augustan age' (ibid.).

Even though such overt congratulatory verse as Gay's addressed to Pope (or even Plomer's addressed to Cavafy) is quite rare these days, dedications like Christopher Reid's as he translates the Sirens episode from the *Odyssey* ('after Homer and for Christopher Logue') serve similar purposes. Sea voyages, moreover, still coincide with moments of inspiration or provide metaphors for what a writer tries to achieve. We see it prominently in the extensive island-hopping that takes place in the Lucas-edited *The Isles of Greece*, as literary sensibilities and cultures come closer in literal or figurative scenes of embarkation and disembarkation. Pytheas himself, the prototypical merchant-explorer, has already been sighted in Kelvin Corcoran's long-standing dialogue with Greek myth and philosophy. This figure is even more extensively considered in Lesley Saunders's sequence *Periplous: The Twelve Voyages of Pytheas*, published as a chapbook in 2016. As an introductory epigraph argues that this circumnavigation, this *periplous*, fixed the British isles 'in the historical imagination as archipelagic, maritime, aloof' (Saunders ibid.: 5), literary endeavours are readily anticipated. Even though Pytheas' own account of the voyage is lost, the back cover points us to a poem which 'attempts to make good that lack, albeit in the consciousness of countless other voyages (imagined as much as real) that have intervened'. First, we share the impressions of the Greek explorer:

> [...]
> Our sails are ripped and sodden,
> we paddle around and around, Kantion
> Belerion Orkas Belerion Orkas
>
> Kantion, the blue tattoo
> of ridge-pines on a too-far mountain,
> the paint of their war-cries,
> the lack of guest ethic, just the salt-
> lick of our fingers no honey
> a knuckle of bread no milk,
>
> hallucinating again
> a woman with dripping hair
> Tethys in her drownedness kelp-like,
> the psychogeography of rapefields
> and scythe-wheeled clearings
> our postcard home.
> ('I. Journey's jargon', ibid.: 6; lines 10-24)

From here, we encounter some sailors involved in the slave trade ('III. Catalogue of ships', ibid.: 10-11), and others positioned in ports in Latin America and the Pacific, 'waiting for work, for women, // for the wind to turn' ('IV. Tanguedad', ibid.: 12-13; lines 24-5), or engaged in piracy ('VIII. Wreck', 20-1) or even experiencing drowning ('IX. Shanty', 22-3). Then we again coast north of the Orkas, to rejoin Pytheas ('XI. Thule', 26-7), whose consciousness soon inhabits the present, and the modern British poet writing about him: 'O I have sailed twenty-three centuries to become her / pacing the bedroom floor cradling / the child skin to skin / rinsing his lotus-bud head in lucid rivulets' ('XII. Nostos', 28-9; lines 20-3).

Just as those missing fragments of Sappho, Aeschylus and Archilochus have energised poetic experiment, as seen elsewhere in this study, it is the absence of Pytheas' account that prompts Saunders – as well as Corcoran before her – to envisage or refashion points of view from the classical world. Scenes from journeys spanning twenty-three centuries can be added to the grid or template of this voyage, alongside anachronisms and snatches from several languages that all confirm to a nautical mindset, Greek or British (or Spanish), but always unquiet and inquiring.

Pytheas is returned to us not only through intertextual glimpses from the *Iliad*, the *Aeneid*, and Avienus' *Ora Maritima*, passages closer to his time embedded in Saunders's sequence in English translation, but also, as the modern poet puts the Anglo-Saxon of *The Seafarer* in the Greek explorer's mouth:

> *I wanna go home ond donne*
> *geþencan hú wé dider cumen*[1]
> the sun dripping through the leaves
> and steam rising off the ship's flank,
> all my iron men singing.
> But we're coasting north of Orkas,
> [...]
> ('XI. Thule', 26; lines 13-8)

If, to recall the comment by Robert Hass cited in the Prologue to this study, the presence of classical Greek poetry suggests a return to powerful origins in the opening of Pound's *Cantos* and, in passing through Latin translation into almost Anglo-Saxon English, also suggests the inexorableness of such dialogues, at the end of Saunders's sequence we arrive at a staging of possibly shared traditions and minds. Here, we are in the company of a more real, and already British, Odysseus. The ventriloquised lines establish similarities and lineage and effect a textual scene of recognition.

Peter Levi, whose work we came across before through his memories and translation of Seferis, wrote an unusual lecture in verse form for his valedictory lecture as Professor of Poetry at the University of Oxford. From this examination of key junctures in literary history, in couplets, certain lines are worth quoting. This is what Levi has to say on orality, on aspects of poetry that were once shared across languages, roles for it inside society, then apparently lost:

> *Though thou the wolf hoar had to priest*
> *though thou him to school set, psalms to learn,*
> *ever be his gears to the grove green.*[2]

---

[1] In her Notes, Saunders provides (2016: 31) the text and translation from the website Anglo-Saxons.net (based on lines 117-8 of the original, rendered there as: 'Let us now ponder where we have a home, / and then think how we will come thither.')

[2] In Levi's 'Notes and References' (1989: 39) he attributes the lines in italics to the '*Oxford Book of English Verse*, no. 278. "Gears" means instinct and habit and inclination'.

> There are true poems, short, real lines like these
> hidden in all natural languages:
> poetry in its first natural state
> is Homeric, tragic, illiterate,
> the shortest and longest of verses
> cluster together where the firelight is,
> and what they have in common is one thing,
> a long line suitable for chanting:
> a line we lost with *Beowulf* and *Gawain*,
> a horn-blast we shall never hear again.
> (*Goodbye to the Art of Poetry*, 1989: 17-8)

We have discussed some of the ways in which British poets like Logue, Hughes and Oswald re-engage classical poetry and drama in an effort to re-install dimensions and methods felt to be lost or disused. What is transmitted and reconfirmed through the *Iliad* in Logue and Oswald, or through Aeschylus and Euripides in Hughes, is a need for a theatrical sense and narrative formations, a renewal of dialogic possibilities. In the case of Oswald especially, we find not only a longing for mutability and a pursuit of it, but also a revaluation of rewarding instabilities of text and the prioritising of performance elements that come through revisiting the oral tradition.

A re-orientation takes place in the modernist project, including making more visible than before intertextual relations at the heart of literary creativity – ones that often align with formative reading experiences. This also leads to a translation that is subjective, *personally inclined* in terms of processes and product. We can trace this attitude back to encounters like Pound's *Cathay* (1915), and, of course, his 1911 version of *The Seafarer*, which Saunders's *Periplous* registers well before it comes to quote the original: Pound's opening lines ('may I for my own self's song truth reckon, / Journey's jargon, how I in harsh days / Hardship endured oft') echo, more than a century later, in the title ('Journey's jargon') that Saunders gives to her first section.

Another legacy of modernism is attention being focused on an increasingly multilingual, or translingual self: thematisations of it, exploring the range of consequences within a poetics. 'The *Volta* project' would be just one among many experiments proceeding from such concerns: Richard Berengarten's poem of the same title from *Black Light* becomes the onset of an online, multilingual anthology (published 2009, as part of issue 9 of *The International Literary Quarterly*). Emerging after a long stay in Greece, the English poem becomes the vehicle for journeys further, rendered now into nearly 100 languages. Though grounded in a specific culture and landscape, it is the splintering into so many voices (from Spanish to Georgian, to Persian and Malay), of a 'Volta' that already strives to interpret Berengarten's surroundings, which precisely assists the original to (re-)encounter its possible meanings. We can count this among the benefits of multiple translation, as Nuala Ní Dhomhnaill has elsewhere argued: 'a plurality of different versions would underline different facets of the original, like differing cuts of a diamond can bring out different lights in the stone' (2003: 90). The poet himself seems aware of possibilities in how theme and treatment may converge, when he writes in his Introduction that

> the setting and take-off point for the poem 'Volta' is an evening walk, a promenade, in a Greek seaside town, as the sun is setting on the horizon. That is: a self-turning, as day is turning into night and as light is evening itself out into darkness. The act of poetic translation too is a 'volta'. And translation involves a turning that is at least double, for it consists of both a return and a departure. (Berengarten 2009)

A multilingual presentation serves to perform, in a collaborative, metatextual space and through a din of languages and dialects, both a variant, changing self and a common humanity. And so implications are already present from the poem's title, before Berengarten then relays his 'Volta' to translators across the globe. Despite distances, they all form a community. (This is even emphasised in that the original has been deliberately placed among the translations, in the correct alphabetical position, as potentially one of them; yet another version.) Their work, in so many languages, over an extended period of time, further serves to express the act of translation as also a shared, long journey. *Translation as adventure.*

On the other hand, modernist impacts in Greek poetry become felt as Seferis variously translates Eliot; his process helps accelerate a transition towards freer verse, as well as longer, episodic structures. Later poets such as Vayenas, Kapsalis, Lagios or Vlavianos explore this landscape further; often situating or anthologising translation work in the course of developing their own preferences and allegiances. In Greek poets writing more recently, closer, 'one on one' relationships are harder to detect, though wider references to Britain and consistent translations of contemporary British poets are made by Orfeas Apergis, Yiannis Doukas Krystalli Glyniadakis, Katerina Iliopoulou, Thodoris Rakopoulos, or Maria Topali – and we do note an increasing alignment in modes of publication and critical discourse between contemporary Greek and Anglophone contexts. When American or Irish poets enter the picture, relationships become even more varied, but until a more comprehensive account emerges, readers may find thoroughly researched perspectives in volumes published by Georganta (2012), and with respect to Irish poetry in particular, Kruczkowska (2017 and forthcoming 2018).

Several examples included in *The Return of Pytheas* suggest ways in which we have moved from a grouping together of 'key names' in the 1960s and 1970s, and the more uncomplicated instances of 'translation-as-presentation' of Greek poetic voices in the decades since, whether individually or in the context of anthologies. At the same time, despite an increasing number of translations of contemporary British poets in literary magazines in Greece, names beyond Hughes are harder to find in book-length editions, despite some exceptions (*Μαύρο Φως*, discussed in chapter 3, is one; and of the other poets included in this book, a Greek edition of Oswald's *Memorial* is forthcoming). Even though many of these translations are by poets, influences arguably either remain unabsorbed or have not yet led to widespread shifts in terms of themes or technique. This is not to seek out, however, some idealised equilibrium; not least as there will always be an unequal reach in terms of the literature produced in the two languages, particularly when English is spoken globally and is the first choice for any poet to be translated into. There is, however, much to accomplish still in improving, coordinating, and deepening, exchanges. Literary festivals for instance, help achieve synchronies of influence; they may foster (translational) dialogues that are closer to 'real time' and can lead to broader awareness in the reading public.

'Hark how the guns salute from either Shore / As thy trim vessel cuts the Thames so fair: / Shouts answering Shouts from Kent and Essex roar' – John Gay exclaims in that eighteenth-century poem, rightly celebrating the arrival his friend Pope makes from 'Homer-land'. For the rest of us, however, there are additional debts and duties; and further, on the ocean, we might imagine Pytheas is still on that ship.

Bibliography

Angelakis, A. 2006. 'Constantine in Constantinople' (trans. J. Lucas), *Modern Poetry in Translation*, Third Series (5): 32-6.

Auden, W. H. 1991. *Collected Poems* (ed. E. Mendelson), New York, NY: Vintage International.

_____. 1984 [1968]. 'The World of Opera'. In *Secondary Worlds: The T. S. Eliot Memorial Lectures Delivered at Eliot College in the University of Kent at Canterbury, October 1967*, London and Boston, MA: Faber and Faber, pp. 76-102.

_____. 1961. 'Introduction'. In *The Complete Poems of Cavafy* (trans. R. Dalven), San Diego, New York, NY and London: Harcourt, pp. xv-xxiii.

Armitage, S. 2017. *The Unaccompanied*, London: Faber and Faber.

_____. 2015. 'Introduction'. In *The Story of the Iliad: A Dramatic Retelling of Homer's Epic and the Last Days of Troy*, New York, NY and London: Liveright Publishing Corporation, pp. v-viii. (British edn: Faber and Faber, 2014)

_____. 2012. *The Death of King Arthur*, London: Faber and Faber.

_____. 2008. *The Odyssey: A Dramatic Retelling of Homer's Epic*, New York, NY: W.W. Norton. (British edn: Faber and Faber, 2006)

_____. 2007. *Sir Gawain and the Green Knight*, New York, NY: W.W. Norton.

_____. 2000. *Mister Heracles: After Euripides*, London: Faber and Faber.

Armitstead, C. 2016. 'Alice Oswald: "I Like the Way that the Death of One Thing is the Beginning of Something Else"', *The Guardian* (22 July). Online at: https://www.theguardian.com/books/2016/jul/22/alice-oswald-interview-falling-awake [accessed 22 August 2017].

Ash, J. 2010. *In the Wake of the Day*, Manchester: Carcanet Press.

_____. 2007. *The Parthian Stations*, Manchester: Carcanet Press.

_____. 2004. *To the City*, Northfield, MA: Talisman House.

_____. 2000. *The Anatolikon*, Northfield, MA: Talisman House.

_____. 1995. *A Byzantine Journey*, New York, NY: Random House.

Balmer, J. 2017a. *The Paths of Survival*, Bristol: Shearsman Books.

_____. 2017b. *Letting Go*, East Sussex: Agenda Editions.

_____. 2013a. *Piecing Together the Fragments: Translating Classical Verse, Creating Contemporary Poetry*, Oxford: Oxford University Press. (Classical Presences)

_____. 2013b. 'Cavafy's Things', *Agenda* 47 (1-2): 90.

_____. 2005. '*The Word for Sorrow*: A Work Begins its Progress', *Modern Poetry in Translation*, Third Series (3): 60-8.

_____. 2004a. *Chasing Catullus: Poems, Translations & Transgressions*, Newcastle upon Tyne: Bloodaxe Books.

_____ (ed. and trans.). 2004b. *Catullus: Poems of Love and Hate*, Newcastle upon Tyne: Bloodaxe Books.

_____. 2003/2004. '*War Music* and *Logue's Homer: All Day Permanent Red* by Christopher Logue', *In Other Words* 22: 78-80.

_____. 1998. 'Alexandria in a Dingy Alleyway: A Version of Cavafy', *Independent on Sunday* (26 July): 26.

_____ (ed. and trans.). 1996. *Classical Women Poets*, Newcastle upon Tyne: Bloodaxe Books.

_____ (ed. and trans.). 1992. *Sappho: Poems and Fragments* (revised edn.), Newcastle upon Tyne: Bloodaxe Books. (first edn.: Brilliance Books, 1984)

Barker, S. 2014. *The Land of Gold*, London: Enitharmon Press.

Barnstone, W. 1993. *The Poetics of Translation: History, Theory, Practice*, New Haven, CT and London: Yale University Press.

Bassnett, S. 2014. 'Variations of Translation'. In *A Companion to Translation Studies* (eds. S. Berman and C. Porter), Oxford: Wiley Blackwell, pp. 54-66.

_____. 2011a. 'Translation or Adaptation?'. In *Reflections on Translation*, Bristol, Buffalo, NY and Toronto: Multilingual Matters, pp. 40-3.

_____. 2011b. 'All in the Mind'. In *Reflections on Translation*, Bristol, Buffalo, NY and Toronto: Multilingual Matters, pp. 74-7.

Berengarten, R. [see also Burns, R.] 2016. *Changing*, Bristol: Shearsman Books.

_____. 2013. *Imagems 1*, Bristol: Shearsman Books.

_____. 2011a. *The Blue Butterfly (The Balkan Trilogy: Part 1)*, Exeter: Shearsman Books.

_____. 2011b. 'The Cambridge Poetry Festival: 35 years after', *Cambridge Literary Review* 1: 148–60. Online at: http://www.cambridgeliteraryreview.org/vol1/issue1/ [accessed 6 May 2017]

_____. 2009. 'Borderlines: An Introduction to the "Volta" Project', *The International Literary Quarterly* 9. Online at: http://interlitRH:org/issue9/berengarten/job.php [accessed 27 December 2016]

Berengarten, R. and Limburg, J. 2017. 'Managing the Art'. In *Richard Berengarten: A Portrait in Inter-Views* (eds. P. Nikolaou and J. Z. Dillon), Bristol: Shearsman Books, pp. 46-80.

Berengarten, R. and Nikolaou, P. 2017. 'Under Greek Light'. In *Richard Berengarten: A Portrait in Inter-Views* (eds. P. Nikolaou and J. Z. Dillon), Bristol: Shearsman Books, pp. 15-45.

_____. 2014. 'Following Black Light', *The International Literary Quarterly* 21. Online at: http://www.interlitq.org/issue21/paschalis-nikolaou/job2.php [accessed 15 March 2017]

Bespaloff, R. 2005. 'On the *Iliad*' (trans. M. McCarthy). In *War and the Iliad: Simone Weil-Rachel Bespaloff*, New York: New York Review Books, pp. 39-63.

Bien, P. et al. (eds.). 2004. *A Century of Greek Poetry 1900-2000*, River Vale, NJ: Cosmos Publishing.

Boland, E. 2012. 'Afterword'. In *Memorial: A Version of Homer's* Iliad by Alice Oswald, New York, NY and London: W. W. Norton, pp. 83-90.

Borges, J.-L. 1998. 'The Immortal'. In *Collected Fictions* (trans. A. Hurley), Harmondsworth: Allen Lane/Penguin, pp. 183-95.

_____. 1939. 'Pierre Menard, autor del Quijote', *Sur* 56: 7-16.

Bowra, C. M. 1957. *The Greek Experience*, Cleveland, OH and New York, NY: The World Publishing Company.

Brown, A. 2016. 'The Tin Lodes', *The Clearing* (26 August). Online at: https://www.littletoller.co.uk/the-clearing/tin-lodes-new-poetry-sequence-andy-brown/ [accessed 18 July 2017].

———. (ed.) 2014. *The Writing Occurs as Song: A Kelvin Corcoran Reader*, Bristol: Shearsman Books.

Burns, R. 2006. [see also Berengarten, R.] *Μαύρο φως. Ποιήματα εις μνήμην Γιώργου Σεφέρη* (*Black Light: Poems in Memory of George Seferis*; bilingual edn., trans. Nasos Vayenas and Ilias Lagios), Athens: Typothito.

———. 2005. *For the Living: Selected Longer Poems 1965–2000*, Cambridge: Salt Publishing.

———. 2003. *Book With No Back Cover*, London: David Paul.

———. 2001. *The Manager*, London and Bath: Elliott and Thompson.

———. 1999. *Against Perfection*, Norwich: The King of Hearts.

———. 1995. *Black Light: Poems in Memory of George Seferis* (3rd edn.), Norwich: The King of Hearts. (1st edn.: Los Poetry Press, 1983)

———. 1972a. *Double Flute*, London: Enitharmon Press.

———. 1972b. *Avebury*, London: Anvil Press Poetry with Routledge and Kegan Paul.

———. 1971. *The Return of Lazarus*, Cambridge: Bragora Press.

——— [Pseudonym: Agnostos Nomolos]. 1968. 'The Easter Rising 1967', poster poem attached to *The London Magazine* 7(10).

Cavafy, C. P. 2017. 'Hidden' (trans. E. Jones). *Poetry Ireland Review* 120: 46.

———. 2015. *Clearing the Ground: Poetry and Prose, 1902-1911* (ed. and trans. M. McKinsey), Chapel Hill, NC: Laertes.

———. 2014. 'Anna Komnene', 'On Italian Shores', 'Apollonius of Tyana on Rhodes' (trans. E. Jones), *Eborakon* 1: 35-8.

———. 2013. *Αποκηρυγμένα. Ποιήματα και μεταφράσεις (1886-1898)* [Repudiated Poems and Translations (1886-1898)], Athens: Ikaros.

———. 2006. 'Two Poems' (trans. J. Manson), *Modern Poetry in Translation*, Third Series (5): 37-9.

———. 2003. *Poems by C. P. Cavafy* (trans. J. C. Cavafy), Athens: Ikaros.

———. 2002. *Πρώτο ταξίδι στην Ελλάδα* [First Journey to Greece], Athens: Roes.

———. 2001. *Before Time Could Change Them: The Complete Poems of Constantine P. Cavafy* (trans. Th. C. Theoharis; foreword G. Vidal), New York, NY: Harcourt.

———. 1961. *The Complete Poems of Cavafy* (trans. R. Dalven; introd. W. H. Auden), London: The Hogarth Press.

———. 1951. *The Poems of C. P. Cavafy* (trans. J. Mavrogordato, introd. R. Warner), London: The Hogarth Press.

Cervantes, M. 1986 [1605-1615]. *The Adventures of Don Quixote de la Mancha* (trans. T. Smollett; introd. C. Fuentes), London: Andre Deutsch.

Chiotis, T. 2015. *Futures: Poetry of the Greek Crisis*, London: Penned in the Margins.

Chiotis, T. and Rossoglou, A. 2017. 'Reading Greece: Theodoros Chiotis on *Futures: Poetry of the Greek Crisis'*, *Greek News Agenda* (4 April). Online at: http://www.greeknewsagenda.gr/index.php/interviews/reading-greece/6360-reading-greece-theodoros-chiotis-on-futures-poetry-of-the-greek-crisis [accessed 28 June 2017].

Connolly, D. 2003. 'Translator's Foreword'. In *Absurd Athlete* by Yannis Kondos, Todmorden: Arc Publications, pp. 12-16. (Visible Poets 11)

Constantine, D. 2004/2005. 'Poetry and Translation: Words from a Poet and Translator', *In Other Words* 24: 39-41.

Cook, E. 2002. 'A Restless and Passionate Engagement', *Poetry London* 43. Online at: http://www.poetrylondon.co.uk/reviews/issue43iii.htm [accessed 22 May 2014].

____. 2001. *Achilles*, London: Methuen.

Corcoran, K. 2017. *Facing West*, Bristol: Shearsman Books.

____. 2015. *Sea Table*, Bristol: Shearsman Books.

____. 2013. *For the Greek Spring*, Bristol: Shearsman Books.

Cunliffe, B. 2001. *The Extraordinary Voyage of Pytheas the Greek: The Man who Discovered Britain*, London: Penguin/Allen Lane.

de Bernières, L. 2013. *Imagining Alexandria*, London: Harvill Secker. eBook.

Dimirouli, F. 2013. 'Rising to Fame: C. P. Cavafy's Journey to Worldwide Recognition'. In *Fame and Glory: The Classic, the Canon and the Literary Pantheon* (eds. J. Goodman and E. Benjamin; MHRA Working Papers in the Humanities, 8), pp. 30-41. Online at: http://www.mhra.org.uk/pdf/wph-8-4.pdf [accessed 19 August 2017].

Doxiadis, A. 2017. *Λέγοντας και ξαναλέγοντας. Η λογοτεχνία, ο μυστηριώδης Πάτροκλος Γιατράς και οι μεταμορφώσεις της Έρημης Χώρας* [Telling and Retelling: Literature, a Mysterious Patroclus Yiatras and the Transformations of *The Waste Land*], Athens: Ikaros.

Drangsholt, J. S. 2016. 'Homecomings: Poetic Reformulations of Dwelling in Jo Shapcott, Alice Oswald, and Lavinia Greenlaw', *Nordic Journal of English Studies* 15(1): 1-23.

Dunn, D. 2003. 'A Dream of Judgment'. In *New Selected Poems 1964-2000*, London: Faber and Faber, p. 23.

Durrell, L. 1980. *Collected Poems 1931-1974* (ed. J. A. Brigham), London: Faber and Faber.

____. 1960. *Clea*, London: Faber and Faber.

____. 1957. *Justine*, London: Faber and Faber.

Dutta, S. 2003. 'Slick Loops of Intestine', *The Daily Telegraph* (16 March). Online at: http://www.arts.telegraph.co.uk/arts/main.jhtml?xml=/arts/2003/03/16/bolog16.xml [accessed 6 December 2015].

Ekdawi, S. 1997. 'Cavafy's English Poems', *Byzantine and Modern Greek Studies* 21(1): 223-30.

____. 2012. 'Definitive Voices of the Loved Dead': Cavafy in English', *Journal of Modern Greek Studies* 30 (1): 129-36.

Eliot, T. S. 1973 [1922]. *The Waste Land*. In *Modern British Literature* (eds. F. Kermode and J. Hollander), New York: Oxford University Press, pp. 474-90. (The Oxford Anthology of English Literature)

Erickson, J. 2003. *The Road to Berlin (Stalin's War with Germany, Volume II)*, London: Cassell Military Paperbacks. (first edn.: Weidenfeld and Nicholson, 1983)

Espiner, M. 2006. 'Troy Story', *The Observer* (22 January): 25.
Eyre, R. 2003. 'My voilà moment', *The Guardian* (12 April). Online at: https://www.theguardian.com/books/2003/apr/12/featuresreviews.guardianreview34 [accessed 2 February 2016].
Ewart, G. 2011. *Selected Poems 1933-1993*, London: Faber and Faber. eBook (Faber Finds).
____. 1980. *The Collected Ewart, 1933-1980*, London: Hutchinson.
Filippakopoulou, M. 2011. 'Foreign in Our Own Country'. In *The Salt Companion to Richard Berengarten* (eds. N. Jope, P. S. Derrick and C. E. Byfield), Cambridge: Salt Publishing, pp. 193-210.
Forster, E. M. 1919. 'The Poetry of C. P. Cavafy', *The Nation and Athenaeum* (25 April), 4643: 247–8.
Fowler, R. 2014. 'Plato, Seferis and Heaney: Poetry as Redress'. In *Re-imagining the Past: Antiquity and Modern Greek Culture* (ed. D. Tziovas), Oxford: Oxford University Press (Classical Presences), pp. 318-29.
Gatsos, N. 1998. *Amorgos* (trans. S. Purcell), London: Anvil Press Poetry.
Georganta, K. 2015. 'A Greek *Waste Land* and the Meta-Writing of History: Elias Lagios' *Erēmē Gē* (1984)', *Comparative Critical Studies* 12(1): 7-25.
____. 2012. *Conversing Identities: Encounters Between British, Irish and Greek Poetry, 1922-1952*, Amsterdam and New York: Rodopi. (TextTtext: Studies in Comparative Literature 67)
____. 2010. '"And so to Athens": William Plomer in "The Land of Love"', *Journal of Modern Greek Studies* 28(1): 49-71.
Gilmour, I. 2002. *The Making of the Poets: Byron and Shelley in Their Time*, New York, NY: Caroll & Graf Publishers.
Goldsworthy, V. 2016. «Ο Άγγελος της Σαλονίκης» (trans. S. Serefas), *Θεσσαλονικέων Πόλις* (March): 98-101.
____. 2015. *Gorsky*, London: Vintage.
____. 2011. *The Angel of Salonika*, Cambridge: Salt Publishing.
____. 2005. *Chernobyl Strawberries*, London: Atlantic Books.
____. 2011. *Inventing Ruritania: The Imperialism of the Imagination*, New Haven, CT: Yale University Press.
Harrison, S. (ed.). 2009. *Living Classics: Greece and Rome in Contemporary Poetry in English*, Oxford: Oxford University Press. (Classical Presences)
Harrison, T. 2016. *Collected Poems*, London: Penguin. (first edn.: Viking, 2007)
Harsent, D. 2012. *In Secret: Versions of Yannis Ritsos*, London: Enitharmon Press.
____. 2010. *Night*, London: Faber and Faber.
Harsent, D. and Miller, G. n.d. 'David Harsent: Night', *Podularity: Authors Talking About Books, Writing, Politics, and More*. Online at: http://podularity.com/wp-content/audio/david%20harsent%20interview%20final.mp3 [accessed 11 May 2017]. Audio Recording.
Hass, R. 2010. 'Introduction'. In *The Greek Poets: Homer to the Present* (eds. P. Constantine et al.), New York: W. W. Norton, pp. ix-xxxiii.
Heaney, S. 2006. *District and Circle*, London: Faber and Faber.
Hoeksema, T. 1978. 'The Translator's Voice: An Interview with Gregory Rabassa', *Translation Review* 1: 5-18.

Hoggard, L. 2006. 'Logue in Vogue', *The Observer* (22 January). Online at: https://www.theguardian.com/books/2006/jan/22/poetry.features [accessed 14 April 2017].

Holman, M. and Boase-Beier, J. 1999. 'Writing, Rewriting and Translation: Through Constraint to Creativity'. In *The Practices of Literary Translation* (eds. J. Boase-Beier and M. Holman), Manchester: St. Jerome, pp. 1-17.

Homer. 2015. *The Iliad: A New Translation* (trans. P. Green), Oakland, CA: University of California Press.

———. 1997. *Iliad* (trans. S. Lombardo), Indianapolis, IN: Hackett Publishing.

———. 1998 [1990]. *The Iliad* (trans. R. Fagles), Harmondsworth: Penguin Books.

———. 1990 [1951]. *The Iliad and the Odyssey of Homer* (trans. R. Lattimore), Chicago, IL: Encyclopaedia Britannica Inc. (Great Books of the Western World, 3).

———. 1897. *The Iliads of Homer, Prince of Poets: Never Before in any Language Truly Translated, Done According to the Greek* (trans. G. Chapman), London: Gibbings.

———. 1715. *The Iliad of Homer* (trans. A. Pope), London: printed by W. Bowyer, for Bernard Lintott et al.

Hughes, T. 2006. *Selected Translations* (ed. D. Weissbort), London: Faber and Faber.

———. 1997. *Tales from Ovid*, London: Faber and Faber.

———. 1999a. *The Oresteia*, London: Faber and Faber.

———. 1999b. *Alcestis*, London: Faber and Faber.

———. 1998. *Birthday Letters*, London: Faber and Faber.

———. 1979. *Moortown Diary*, London: Faber and Faber.

———. 1967. *Lupercal*, London: Faber and Faber.

Jeffreys, P. (ed.). 2009. *The Forster-Cavafy Letters: Friends at a Slight Angle*, Cairo and New York; The American University in Cairo Press.

Jones, E. 2016a. 'Later Emperors', *PN Review* 232 (43/2): 25-6.

———. 2016b. 'Evan Jones on C. P. Cavafy', *Eborakon* (Special Online Issue: European Poetry). Online at: https://www.eborakon.com/special-online-issue-europe/e-jones-on-c-p-cavafy/ [accessed 25 February 2017].

———. 2012. *Paralogues*, Manchester: Carcanet Press.

———. 2011. 'Cavafian Melancholy in Don Paterson and A. E. Stallings'. Paper delivered at the International Conference *Poetry and Melancholia*, University of Stirling (8-10 July).

Jones, E. and Campbell, J. 2012. 'Interview with Evan Jones', *Maisonneuve: A Quarterly of Arts, Opinion & Ideas* (30 November). Online at: https://maisonneuve.org/article/2012/11/30/interview-evan-jones/ [accessed July 3, 2017].

Jung, C. G. 1961. *Septem Sermones ad Mortuos* (trans. H. G. Baynes), London: Stuart and Watkins.

Kampanellis, I. 1965. *Μαουτχάουζεν* [The Mauthausen Chronicle], Athens: Themelio.

Katope, C. G. 1969. 'Cavafy and Durrell's *The Alexandria Quartet*', *Comparative Literature* 21(2): 125-37.

Kavounas, A. 2017. *Abandoned Gardens: Selected & New Poems*, Bristol: Shearsman Books.

_____. 2009. *Ornament of Asia*, Exeter: Shearsman Books.

_____. 1995. *The Invited*, London: Sinclair-Stevenson.

Kavounas, A. and Kennedy, J. 2014. 'Shearsman poet Alice Kavounas and Apple developer John Kennedy describe their collaboration and creation of a location-based app *Words in Air: Poetry-in-Place*', *Londongrip.co.uk: The International Online Poetry Magazine*. Online at https://londongrip.co.uk/2014/04/words-in-air-out-of-thin-air/ [accessed 9 July 2017].

Keeley, E. and Sherrard, P. 1981. 'Introduction'. In *Odysseus Elytis: Selected Poems* (eds. and trans. E. Keeley and P. Sherrard), London: Anvil Press Poetry, pp. ix-xiv.

_____ (eds). 1966. *Four Greek Poets: C. P. Cavafy – George Seferis – Odysseus Elytis – Nikos Gatsos*, London: Penguin Books. (Penguin Modern European Poets 91)

Kruczkowska, J. (ed.). forthcoming 2018. *Landscapes of Irish and Greek Poets: Essays, Poems, Interviews*, Oxford: Peter Lang.

_____ 2017. *Irish Poets and Modern Greece: Heaney, Mahon, Cavafy, Seferis*, London: Palgrave Macmillan.

Lagios, E. 2014. *Erēmē Gē* (trans. K. Georganta), *Modern Greek Studies Online* 1: [T]1-23. Online at: http://www.moderngreek.org.uk/journal/sites/default/files/articles/MGSO_vol_1_(2015).pdf [accessed 3 June 2017].

Letsios, V. 2011. «Το ποιητικό θέατρο, το *Φονικό στην Εκκλησιά* και η μετάφραση του Σεφέρη» [Verse Drama, *Murder in the Cathedral* and Seferis's Translation], *Πόρφυρας* 139: 16-26.

Levi, P. 1989. *Goodbye to the Art of Poetry*, London: Anvil Press Poetry.

_____. 1980. *The Hill of Kronos*, London: Collins.

Leviston, F. 2013. '*For the Greek Spring* by Kelvin Corcoran – review', *The Guardian* (12 October). Online at: https://www.theguardian.com/books/2013/oct/18/greek-spring-kelvin-corcoran-review [accessed July 5, 2017].

Lewis, W. 1937. *Blasting and Bombardiering*, London: Eyre & Spottiswoode.

Limburg, J. 2002. 'Human Above All: Richard Burns's *The Manager*', *The Jewish Quarterly* 185: 7-23.

Logue, C. 2015. *War Music* (ed. C. Reid), London: Faber and Faber.

_____. 2005. *Cold Calls: War Music continued*, London: Faber and Faber.

_____. 2003a. *All Day Permanent Red: War Music continued*, London: Faber and Faber.

_____. 2003b. 'The Shortest Long Poem Ever Written: An Interview with Christopher Logue', *Areté* 13: 117-36.

_____. 2001. *War Music: An Account of Books 1-4 and 16-19 of Homer's Iliad*, London: Faber and Faber.

_____. 1999. *Prince Charming: A Memoir*, London: Faber and Faber.

_____. 1996. *Selected Poems* (ed. C. Reid), London: Faber and Faber.

_____. 1994. *The Husbands*, London: Faber and Faber.

_____. 1991. *Kings*, New York, NY: Farrar, Straus and Giroux.

_____. 1981. *War Music: An Account of Books 16 to 19 of Homer's Iliad*, London: Jonathan Cape.

____. 1967. *Pax*, London: Rapp & Carroll.

____. 1962. *Patrocleia*, London: Scorpion Press.

Logue, C., and Guppy, S. 1993. 'The Art of Poetry No. 66', *The Paris Review* 127: 238-64. Online at: https://www.theparis-review.org/interviews/1929/christopher-logue-the-art-of-poetry-no66-christopher-logue [accessed 6 November 2015].

Lucas, J. (ed.) 2010. *The Isles of Greece: A Collection of the Poetry of Place*, London: Eland Publishing.

MacAuliffe, J. 2012. 'The Future Past: Evan Jones' Paralogues and Cavafy', *Carcanet Blog* (29 January). Online at: http://carcanetblog.blogspot.gr/2012/06/future-past-evan-jones-paralogues-and.html [accessed May 14, 2017].

MacKay, M. 2017. *Modernism, War, and Violence*, London: Bloomsbury. (New Modernisms)

Malanos, T. 1981. «Μια συνοπτική παρουσίαση του Καβάφη» [A Concise Account of Cavafy]. In *Ο Καβάφης απαραμόρφωτος* [Cavafy Undistorted], Athens: Prosperos, pp. 7-20.

____. 1957. *Ο ποιητής Κ. Π. Καβάφης. Ο άνθρωπος και το έργο του* [The Poet C. P. Cavafy: The Man and His Work], Athens: Difros. (first edn.: Govostis 1933)

Malli, M. 2004. «Ο Νάσος Βαγενάς ως μεταμοντέρνος ποιητής» [Nasos Vayenas as a Postmodern Poet]. In *Νάσος Βαγενάς. Μελετήματα* [Studies on Nasos Vayenas] (ed. Th. Pylarinos), Athens: Vivliothiki Trapezas Attikis, pp. 31-56.

____. 2002. *Μοντερνισμός, μεταμοντερνισμός και περιφέρεια. Μια μελέτη της μεταφραστικής θεωρίας και πρακτικής του Νάσου Βαγενά* [Modernism, Postmodernism and Periphery: A Study of the Translation Theory and Practice of Nasos Vayenas], Athens: Polis.

Manguel, A. 2008. 'The Books of Don Quixote'. In *The City of Words*, London & New York, NY: Continuum, pp. 87-115.

Mendelsohn, D. 2009. 'The Poet-Historian'. In *C. P. Cavafy: Collected Poems*, New York, NY: Alfred A. Knopf, pp. xv-lix.

Middleton, C. 2014. *Collected Later Poems*, Manchester: Carcanet Press. eBook.

____. 2005. 'A Retrospective Sketch', *Chicago Review* 51(1-2): 11-16.

____. 1963. 'What Could You Have Made of it, Kavafis?', *The Carleton Miscellany* 4(1): 101.

Moore, K. 2015. *The Art of Falling*, Bridgend: Seren Books.

Morgan, K. 1977. *Ovid and the Art of Imitation: Propertius in the Amores*, Leiden: E. J. Brill.

Ní Dhomhnaill, N. 2003. 'Linguistic Ecology: Preventing a Great Loss'. In *Lives in Translation: Bilingual Writers on Identity and Creativity* (ed. I. de Courtivron), New York, NY: Palgrave Macmillan, pp. 79-91.

Nikolaou, P. (ed.). 2015. *12 Greek Poems after Cavafy*, Bristol: Shearsman Books.

____. 2008. 'Turning Inward: Literary Translation and Life-Writing'. In *Translating Selves: Experience and Identity between Languages and Literatures* (eds. P. Nikolaou and M.-V. Kyritsi), London and New York, NY: Continuum, pp. 53-70.

____. 2006a. *The Translating Self: Literary Translation and Life-Writing*. PhD thesis, University of East Anglia, Norwich, UK.

____. 2006b. 'Richard Burns – *Black Light: Poems in Memory of George Seferis*', *Modern Poetry in Translation* Third Series (5): 168-71.

Norris, M. 2000. *Writing War in the Twentieth Century*, Charlottesville, VA and London: University of Virginia Press.

Oswald, A. 2016. *Falling Awake*, London: Jonathan Cape.

____. 2012. *Memorial: A Version of Homer's Iliad*, New York, NY and London: W. W. Norton.

____. 2011a. *Memorial: An Excavation of the Iliad*, London: Faber and Faber.

____. 2011b. 'The Unbearable Brightness of Speaking', *New Statesman* (17 October). Online at: http://www.newstatesman.com/books/2011/10/homer-essay-iliad-poetry-poem [accessed 2 March 2017].

____. 2011c. *Memorial: Read by Alice Oswald*, London: Faber and Faber. Audio Recording.

____. 2005. 'Wild Things', *The Guardian* (2 December). Online at: https://www.theguardian.com/books/2005/dec/03/poetry.tedhughes [accessed 7 May 2017].

____. 2002. *Dart*, London: Faber and Faber.

Oswald, A. and Porter, M. 2014. 'Interview with Alice Oswald', *The White Review* 11. Online at: http://www.thewhitereview.org/interviews/interview-with-alice-oswald/ [accessed 3 February 2017].

Ovid. 1994. *The Poems of Exile* (trans. P. Green), London: Penguin. (Penguin Classics)

Papageorgiou, F. 2017. *The Purloined Letter*, Bristol: Shearsman Books.

____. 2015. *Not So Ill with You and Me*, Bristol: Shearsman Books.

Paterson, D. 2009. *Rain*, London: Faber and Faber.

____. 2006. 'Fourteen Notes on the Version'. In *Orpheus: A Version of Rilke's Die Sonette an Orpheus*, London: Faber and Faber, pp. 73-84.

____. 2003. *Landing Light*, London: Faber and Faber.

Paz, O. 1997. *A Tale of Two Gardens: Poems from India 1952-1995* (ed. and trans. E. Weinberger), New York, NY: New Directions.

Pentzikis, G. 2005. *Πάτροκλος Γιατράς. Ένας ποιητικός ήρωας του Νάσου Βαγενά – οι δυο πόλοι ενός προσωπείου.* [Patroclus Yiatras: A Poetical Hero of Nasos Vayenas –Two Poles of a Persona], Athens: Sokoli.

Pinchin, J. L. 1977. *Alexandria Still: Forster, Durrell, and Cavafy*, Princeton, NJ: Princeton University Press. (Princeton Studies in Literature)

Plomer, W. 1932. *The Fivefold Screen*, London: Hogarth Press.

Pound, E. 1992. 'Guido's Relations'. In *Theories of Translation: An Anthology of Essays from Dryden to Derrida* (eds. R. Schulte and J. Biguenet), Chicago, IL: University of Chicago Press, pp. 83-92.

____. 1988. *The Cantos*, London: Faber and Faber.

____. 1948. *Selected Poems* (introd. T. S. Eliot), London: Faber and Faber.

____. 1934 [1919]. *Homage to Sextus Propertius*, London: Faber and Faber.

____. 1915. *Cathay*, London: Elkin Mathews.

———. 1911. 'The Seafarer', *New Age* 10 (5): 107.
Rayor, D. J. 2016. 'Translating Sappho: Songs, Poems, Fragments', *Translation Review* 94: 28-41.
———. 1990. 'Translating Fragments', *Translation Review* 32-3: 15-18.
Reid, C. 2015. *The Curiosities*, London: Faber and Faber.
———. 2003. *For and After*, London: Faber and Faber.
———. 1985. *Katerina Brac*, London: Faber and Faber.
Reynolds, M. 2011. *The Poetry of Translation: From Chaucer & Petrarch to Homer & Logue*, Oxford: Oxford University Press.
Ricks, D. 2007. '"A faint sweetness in the never-ending afternoon"? Reflections on Cavafy and the Greek epigram', *Κάμπος: Cambridge Papers in Modern Greek* 15: 149-69.
———. 2004. 'Cavafy's Alexandrianism'. In *Alexandria Real or Imagined* (eds. A. Hirst and M. Silk), Aldershot: Ashgate, pp. 337-51.
———. 2002. 'Cavafy's Stationary', *Poetry*, June issue: 147.
———. 1993. 'Cavafy Translated', *Κάμπος: Cambridge Papers in Modern Greek* 1: 85-110.
———. 1989. *The Shade of Homer: A Study in Modern Greek Poetry*, Cambridge: Cambridge University Press.
Riley, P. 2014. 'Kelvin Corcoran and Greece'. In *The Writing Occurs as Song: A Kelvin Corcoran Reader* (ed. A. Brown), Bristol: Shearsman Books, pp. 74-89.
———. 2009. *Greek Passages*, Exeter: Shearsman Books.
Samarakis, A. 1969. *The Flaw* (trans. P. Mansfield and R. Burns), London: Hutchinson; New York, NY: Weybright and Talley.
Saunders, L. 2016. *Periplous: The Twelve Voyages of Pytheas*, Bristol: Shearsman Books.
Schrott, R. 2011. 'Marsala', 'Pulchra et Luna', 'Actaeon', 'La Cuba' (trans. E. Jones), *Studio: Online Literary Journal*, 5(1). Online at: http://studiojournal.ca/vol-5-1-2011/translation/jones/poem3/index.html [accessed 7 August 2017].
Scott, C. 2000. *Translating Baudelaire*, Exeter: University of Exeter Press.
Seferis, G. 2014. *Ποιήματα* [Poems] (ed. D. Daskalopoulos), Athens: Ikaros.
———. 1966. *On the Greek Style: Selected Essays in Poetry and Hellenism* (trans. R. Warner and Th. D. Frangopoulos), Boston, MA: Atlantic – Little, Brown.
Sinfield, A. 1997. *Literature, Politics and Culture in Postwar Britain*, London and Atlantic Highlands, NJ: The Athlone Press.
Sotiripoulos, E. 2015. *Τι μένει από τη νύχτα* [What's Left of the Night], Athens: Patakis.
Steiner, G. 1996. 'Homer in English'. In *No Passion Spent: Essays 1978-1995*, London: Faber and Faber, pp. 88-107.
——— (ed.). 1970. *Poem into Poem: World Poetry in Modern Verse Translation*, Harmondsworth: Penguin.
Stopa-Hunt, C. 2012. 'Visible Vanishing', *The Oxonian Review* 18(5). Online at: http://www.oxonianreview.org/wp/visible-vanishing/ [accessed 12 August 2017].

Sullivan, J. P. 1964. *Ezra Pound and Sextus Propertius: A Study in Creative Translation*, London: Faber and Faber.

Tatum, J. 2003. *The Mourner's Song: War and Remembrance from the Iliad to Vietnam*, Chicago, IL and London: University of Chicago Press.

Thacker, J. P. 2015. 'The Thing in the Gap-Stone Style: Alice Oswald's Acoustic Arrangements', *Cambridge Quarterly* 44(2): 103-18.

The Hypatia Trust. 2013. 'A Poetry app for you to try!' (20 May). Online at: http://hypatia-trust.org.uk/blog/2013/05/20/a-poetry-app-for-you-to-try [accessed 7 January 2017].

Thwaite, A. 1995. 'Obituary: Gavin Ewart', *The Independent* (24 October). Online at: http://www.independent.co.uk/news/people/obituary-gavin-ewart-1579164.html [accessed 4 July 2017].

Tomlinson, C. 2003. *Metamorphoses: Poetry and Translation*, Manchester: Carcanet Press.

Trypanis, C. A. (ed.). 1951. *Medieval and Modern Greek Poetry: An Anthology*, Oxford: Clarendon Press.

Tziovas, D. 2005. 'Review of Bien, P. et al., *A Century of Greek Poetry 1900-2000*', *Journal of Modern Greek Studies* 23(2): 406-8.

Underwood, S. 1998. *English Translators of Homer: from George Chapman to Christopher Logue*, Plymouth: Northcote House, in association with the British Council. (Writers and their Work)

Van Dyck, K. 2016. 'Introduction'. In *Austerity Measures: The New Greek Poetry*, London and New York, NY: Penguin, pp. xvii-xxv.

____. 1998. *Cassandra and the Censors: Greek Poetry Since 1967*, Ithaca and London: Cornell University Press.

Vassar Info. 2014. 'Words in Air' (News; 26 February). Online at: https://info.vassar.edu/news/features/2013-2014/140226-words-in-air.html [accessed 30 October 2016].

Vayenas, N. 2010. *The Perfect Order: Selected Poems 1974-2010* (eds. R. Berengarten and P. Nikolaou), London: Anvil Press Poetry.

____. 2010b. *Στη νήσο των Μακάρων* [On the Isle of the Blest]. Athens: Kedros.

____. 2010c. 'Cavafy's Poetry of Irony' (trans. J. Davis). In *The Perfect Order: Selected Poems 1974-2010*, (eds. R. Berengarten and P. Nikolaou), London: Anvil Press Poetry, pp. 133-6.

____. 2001a. *Σκοτεινές μπαλλάντες και άλλα ποιήματα* [Dark Ballads and Other Poems], Athens: Kedros.

____. 2001b. «Η κρίση του ελεύθερου στίχου» [The Crisis of Free Verse], *Nea Estia* 1734: 721-7.

____ (ed.) 2000. *Συνομιλώντας με τον Καβάφη. Ανθολογία ξένων καβαφογενών ποιημάτων* [Conversing with Cavafy: An Anthology of Foreign Cavafy-inspired Poems], Thessaloniki: Kentro Ellinikis Glossas.

____. 1997. *Η πτώση του ιπτάμενου, β΄* [Flyer's Fall, II], Athens: Parousia.

____. 1989a. *Η πτώση του ιπτάμενου* [Flyer's Fall], Athens: Stigmi.

____. 1989b. «Ο Σεφέρης ως μεταφραστής της αγγλικής ποίησης» [Seferis as a Translator of English Poetry]. In *Ποίηση και μετάφραση* [Poetry and Translation], Athens: Stigmi, pp. 95-100.

_____. 1979. *Ο ποιητής και ο χορευτής. Μια εξέταση της ποιητικής και της ποίησης του Σεφέρη* [The Poet and the Dancer: A Study of the Poetics and Poetry of Seferis], Athens: Kedros.
_____. 1978. *Βιογραφία* [Biography], Athens: Kedros.
_____. 1976. «Πάτροκλος Γιατράς, ή Οι Ελληνικές μεταφράσεις της *Έρημης Χώρας*» ['Patroclus Yiatras, or, the Greek Translations of *The Waste Land*']. In *Η συντεχνία* [The Guild], Athens: Stigmi, pp. 2-20.
Vayenas, N. and Stefanidis, M. 2009. «Ο ποιητής είναι τρόπος, δεν είναι δήλωση» [Deeds, not statements, define the poet], *Se Eniko Arithmo me ton Mano Stephanidi* (24 February). Online at: http://manosstefanidis.blogspot.gr/2009/02/blog-post_9469.html [accessed 28 April 2016].
Venuti, L. 2013. 'Teaching in Translation'. In *Translation Changes Everything: Theory and Practice*, London and New York, NY: Routledge, pp. 165-72.
Yao, S. G. 2010. 'Translation'. In *Ezra Pound in Context* (ed. I. B. Nadel), Cambridge: Cambridge University Press, pp. 33-42.
_____. 2003. *Translation and the Languages of Modernism: Gender, Politics, Language*, London and New York, NY: Palgrave Macmillan.

Digital Resources

The Cavafy Archive: <http://www.cavafy.com/>
The Paths of Survival: <https://thepathsofsurvival.wordpress.com/josephine-balmer/>
Volta: A Multilingual Anthology: <http://interlitq.org/issue9/volta/job.php>
Words in Air: Poetry in Place <https://itunes.apple.com/us/app/words-in-air-uk-edition/id566902258?mt=8&ign-mpt=uo%3D2>

Index

Achilles 9, 28, 35, 39, 59, 122
Aeschylus 42, 62, 131, 133
   Myrmidons 58, 59, 121, 122
   The Oresteia (trans. Hughes) 42
Afghanistan 41
Aldermaston March (1958) 27
Alexandria 104, 120
Alexandroupolis 111
Amphipolis 111
anachronisms 32, 34, 47, 97, 131
Angelakis, Andreas, 'Constantine in Constantinople' 119
Anghelaki-Rooke, Katerina 74
anthologies 11–15, 46, 58, 90, 91, 100, 113, 115, 126, 133–5
anti-Semitism 25
anti-war movement 17, 25, 26, 28
Apergis, Orfeas 135
Apollinaire, Guillaume 118
Apple, iTunes store 109
Archilochus (Archilochos) 99–100, 131
Aretè 32, 36
Aristophanes, *Assemblywomen* 58
Armitage, Simon 48
   The Death of King Arthur 47
   The Last Days of Troy 47
   Mister Heracles 46
   The Odyssey: A Dramatic Retelling of Homer's Epic 46–7
   'Poundland' 47
   Sir Gawain and the Green Knight 47
   The Unaccompanied 47
Armitstead, Claire 65, 67
Ash, John 125–9
   The Anatolikon 125
   'The Antiochiad' 126
   (trans.) 'Antiochus Epiphanes' (Cavafy) 126n
   (trans.) 'The Battle of Magnesia' (Cavafy) 126, 126n
   'The Bergamot Tree' 126
   (trans.) 'The Bishop's Assurances' (Cavafy) 126
   A Byzantine Journey 125

   (trans.) 'A Byzantine Nobleman Writing in Exile' (Cavafy) 126n
   (trans.) 'Disillusionment of Demetrius Soter' (Cavafy) 126n
   'Displeasure of Ruins' 125
   (trans.) 'Exiles' (Cavafy) 126n
   (trans.) 'Fever of Kleitos' (Cavafy) 126n, 126–7, 128–9
   (trans.) 'The Gods in their Wisdom' (Cavafy) 126n
   (trans.) 'In Ösroene' (Cavafy) 126n
   (trans.) 'In a Syrian Harbour' (Cavafy) 126n
   In the Wake of the Day 125
   (trans.) 'A Maker of Mixing Bowls (Cavafy) 126
   (trans.) '2. Of Coloured Glass' (Cavafy) 126
   'The Names of Kings' 125
   The Parthian Stations 125
   (trans.) 'Sorrow of Macedon' (Cavafy) 126
   To the City 125
   (trans.) 'The Triumph of John Kantakouzenos' (Cavafy) 126, 126n
   (trans.) 'Without Memorial' (Cavafy) 126, 126n
   'The Women of Kars' 126
Athens 71
atomic bomb 84
Auden, W. H. 16, 89, 115, 129
   'Atlantis' 112
   The Bassarids 43
   'Rois Fainéants' 112
   Secondary Worlds 43
   'The Shield of Achilles' 18
auditory imagination 68
Auschwitz 84
Avienus, *Ora Maritima* 132

Baghdad 58
Balkans 72, 104, 106
Balmer, Darlene 60–1
Balmer, Josephine 22, 48, 49–62

'Aeschylus' Revision' 58
'Breaking the Pact' 60
'By-pass' 60
(ed. and trans.) *Catullus: Poems of Love and Hate* 49, 57
'Cavafy's Things' 120
Chasing Catullus: Translations and Transgressions 49, 50, 55, 57, 57–8, 60, 120
(ed. and trans.) *Classical Women Poets* 49
'Digging In' 55
'Erotic Tales' 59–60
'Fairfield Church' 60
'Greek Tragedy' 50
'Knocking at the Door' 54
'Letting Go' 60, 121
'Market Overton' 60
'Naso Sees Action' 55
'Naso Writes his Own Epitaph' 54
'The Other Path' 60
The Paths of Survival 59, 121
'Philomela' 50–1
Piecing Together the Fragments 56, 120
(ed. and trans.) *Sappho: Poems and Fragments* 49
'Sarpedon's Version' 121–22, 128
'Seat' 61
'"78 Nights' 119–20
'Snow' 61
'Sources and Notes' 60, 61
'Spring' 61
'The Things We Leave Behind' 120–1
'The Word for Sorrow' 51, 52, 58
Baltic region 9
Barker, Sebastian 72, 100, 103, 111
'A Cocktail on Cos' 101
The Land of Gold 100
'A Monastery of Light' 100, 101
'Sitochóri' 100
'The Sitochori Poems. A Village in the Mountains of the south-west Peloponnese' 100
Barnstone, Willis, *The Poetics of Translation* 22
Basilides of Alexandria 75
Bassnett, Susan 41, 42, 106–7
Baudelaire, Charles 83

BBC 17
  Radio 120
  Third Programme 41
  World Service 107
Beckett, Samuel
  Breath 67
  Footfalls 67
Bellou, Sotiria 75
Beowulf 133
Berengarten, Richard 71–75, 100, 103, 107, 111
  Against Perfection 73
  as 'Agnostos Nomolos' 71n
  The Blue Butterfly 73
  Changing 73
  Nada: Hope or Nothing 74
  'An Old Man in the Harbour' 80
  'Only the Common Miracle' 77
  'Volta: A Multilingual Anthology' 133–4
  see also Burns, Richard
Bespaloff, Rachel 28, 36
Bible, versions of 77
Bien, P. et al. (eds.), *A Century of Greek Poetry 1900–2000* 13
bilingualism 83
Bishop, Elizabeth 109
Black Watch regiment 26
Blake, William 76, 77, 109
Boase-Beier, Jean 82
Boland, Eavan 65, 69
Borges, Jorge Luis 17, 84, 87
Bosphorus 48
Bowra, C. M., *The Greek Experience* 78
Brecht, Bertolt 27
Britain 9, 26, 135
  see also United Kingdom
Broome, William 130
Brown, Andy
  'The Tin Lodes' 97n
  (ed.) *The Writing Occurs as Song: A Kelvin Corcoran Reader* 94
Bulgaria 111
Burns, Richard (Richard Berengarten)
  Avebury 74, 75
  Black Light: Poems in Memory of George Seferis 77–81, 82, 85, 133

149

'Cicadas (I)' 79
'Cicadas (II)' 78
'In Memory of George Seferis' 79
Book with No Back Cover 75
Double Flute 72
'The Easter Rising 1967' 71n
'Eleftheria' 71, 72
For the Living: Longer Poems 1965–2000 71n, 72
'The Funeral' 72
'In his Ancestral Garden' 72
Learning to Talk 72, 73
'Male Figure Playing a Double Flute' 72
The Manager 72, 74, 76, 77
'Notes and Acknowledgments' 79
'Ode on the End of the Third Exile' 72–3
The Return of Lazarus 71, 72, 75, 77
'Shell' 79
'Three Songs of Exile' 72
'Zeimbekiko' 72, 75
Μαύρο Φως. Ποιήματα εις μνήμην Γιώργου Σεφέρη (trans. Vayenas & Lagios) 79, 135
Byron, George Gordon, Lord 96
Byzantine era 72, 98, 118, 125

Calvos, Andreas 83
Cambridge 78
    Poetry Festival 74
Campaign for Nuclear Disarmament (CND) 27
Cape Sounion 91–2
The Carleton Miscellany 124
Carne-Ross, Donald 17, 27, 28, 69
    'On Homer' 22
Carson, Anne 56
Catullus 53, 57
Cavafy, C. P. 10, 16, 60, 83, 103, 103n, 104, 112–29, 130
    diary 91
    irony in 114
    'Afternoon Sun' (trans. Harsent) 124
    'The Afternoon Sun' 113
    'Alexandrian Kings' 112, 116
    'Anna Komnene' (trans. Jones) 119
    'Antiochus Epiphanes' (trans. Ash) 126n
    'Apollonius of Tyana on Rhodes' (trans. Jones) 119
    'The Art of Poetry' (trans. Harsent) 124
    'At the Tobacconist's Window' (trans. Harsent) 124
    'The Battle of Magnesia' 124
    'The Battle of Magnesia' (trans. Ash) 126, 126n
    'The Bandaged Shoulder' (trans. Paterson) 123
    'Before Time Could Change Them' (trans. Reid, 'The Circumstances') 123
    'The Bishop's Assurances' (trans. Ash) 126
    'The Boat' (trans. Paterson) 123
    'The Bowl-Maker' (trans. Paterson) 123
    'A Byzantine Nobleman Writing in Exile' (trans. Ash) 126n
    'Che Fece… Il Gran Rifiuto' 113
    'Of Coloured Glass' (trans. Ash) 126
    The Complete Poems of Cavafy (trans. Rae Dalven, intro. W.H. Auden) 16, 112
    'Darius' 116
    'Darkness and Shadows' 115
    'Disillusionment of Demetrius Soter' (trans. Ash) 126n
    'Exiles' (trans. Ash) 126n
    'Far Away' 113
    'Fever of Kleitos' (trans. Ash) 126n, 126–8, 129
    'Finalities' 123
    'For Ammones Who Died at the Age of 29 in 610' 116
    'The God Abandons Antony' (trans. Durrell) 113
    'The Gods in their Wisdom' (trans. Ash) 126n
    'Hidden' (trans. Jones) 119
    'In a Famous Greek Colony, 200 B.C.' 123
    'In Osroene' (trans. Ash) 126n
    'In a Syrian Harbour' (trans. Ash) 126n
    'In the Port' (trans. Jones) 119
    'Ithaca' 116
    'Leaving Therapia' 115

'A Maker of Mixing Bowls' (trans. Ash) 126
'(More Happy Thou, Performing Member)' 115
'Myres: Alexandria A.D. 340' 128
'On Italian Shores' (trans. Jones) 119
'One Night' (trans. Paterson) 123
The Poems of C.P. Cavafy (trans. J. Mavrogordato, introd. R. Warner) 112
'Two Poems' (trans. J. Manson) 119
'Sorrow of Macedon' (trans. Ash) 126
'The Triumph of John Kantakouzenos' (trans. Ash) 126, 126n
'Without Memorial' (trans. Ash) 126n
'Η Αρρώστια του Κλείτου' 124–5
Cavafy, John 115
The Cavafy Archive 115
Cavalcanti, Guido 23
Caxton, William 18
Cervantes, Miguel de 87
Chapman, George 17, 18, 18–19, 22
Chiotis, Theodoros (ed.), *Futures: Poetry of the Greek Crisis* 15
cinema 13, 22, 33, 48
civil disobedience 26
Classicism 118
Cold War 27
Coleridge, Samuel Taylor 109
Committee of 100, 26, 28
Connolly, David 11
Constantine, David 44n, 92
Constantine, Helen 44n
Constantine, Peter, et al, (eds) *The Greek Poets: Homer to the Present* 10, 12–13
Cook, Elizabeth, *Achilles* 39
Corcoran, Kelvin 72, 94–99, 103, 107, 111, 130, 131
   'Alexiares in Exile' 97
   'And Coming Back' 98
   'Apokriatika' 95
   'Byron's Karagiozis' 96
   'Dionysus' 99
   'Elizabeth Bishop' 98
   'Epicurus Is My Neighbour' 97
   Facing West 99
   'Footnote to the Above' 99
   For the Greek Spring 94, 97
   'News of Aristomenes' 97
   'The Objects Were not Paid for or Got for a Fixed Price (Elgin)' 96
   Radio Archilochos 99–100
   'Sappho' 98
   Sea Table 98, 99
   'Three Monologues' 97
   'The Ingliss Touriste Patient' 98
   'Pytheas' 97–8
Corinth 95
Cornwall 61
   Housel Bay 110
   Lizard Peninsula 107
   Coverack 107
Cowper, William 18, 56
Criterion 116
Cunliffe, Barry, *The Extraordinary Voyage of Pytheas the Greek: The Man Who Discovered Britain* 9, 97
Cycladic sculpture 75
Cyprus 91

Dalven, Rae 16
Dante Alighieri, *The Divine Comedy* 63
Dardanelles (Hellespont) 48, 51
Dart, river 68, 97n
Davis, Paul, *Translation and the Poet's Life: The Ethics of Translating in English Culture, 1646–1726* 130
Dawkins, R. N. 16
de Bernières, Louis 121
   'Charity Function' 117
   'For One Night Only' 117
   Imagining Alexandria 117
   'Romance' 117
Delos 75
Dicaearchus 9
Doukas, Yiannis 135
Doxiadis, Apostolos 87
Drangsholt, Janne Stigen 68
Dryden, John 18
Dugdale, Sasha 44n
Dunn, Douglas, 'A Dream of Judgment' 82
Durnin, John 42
Durrell, Laurence 124
   'Cavafy' 112–113
   Clea 113
   Collected Poems, 1931–1974 113

Justine 113
    (trans.) 'The God Abandons Antony'
        (Cavafy) 113
Dutta, Shomit 39–40

East Anglia, University of 103
Eborakon 119
Edgehill, Battle of 32
El Alamein, Battle of 31
Eliot, T. S. 24, 36, 43, 48, 52, 68, 89, 102,
    116, 124, 134
    Murder in the Cathedral 83
    The Waste Land 10, 83, 85–6, 87, 97n
Elizabethan poetry 76
Elpenor 47
Elytis, Odysseus 75, 100, 103n
    'The Autopsy' 100
    'The Light Tree' 100
    'The Other Noah' 100
    Selected Poems 12–13
Embiricos, Andreas 103n
English language 12, 42
Engonopoulos, Nikos 103n
Ennius 53
Erickson, John, *The Road to Berlin (Stalin's
    War with Germany, Volume II* 31
Espiner, M. 35
Euripides 42, 49, 62, 133
    Alcestis (trans. Hughes) 42, 63
    Heracles 46
    Medea 50, 51
Evros, river 111
Ewart, Gavin 88
    obituary 89–91
    'A Ballad Re-Creation of a Fifties
        Incident at Barnes Bridge' 90
    'Climacteric' 87
    'Home Truths' 88
    Londoners, 89
    'A Personal Footnote' 87
    'Poets' 88–9
    'Sestina: The Literary Gathering' 90
    'Sonnet: Afterwards' 90
    'The Select Party' 87
    '2001: The Tennyson/Hardy Poem' 89
Exeter, University of 103
Eyre, Richard 34

Faas, Egbert 41
Faber and Faber 46
Fagles, Robert 19
favourite words 32
festivals, literary 135
Filippakopoulou, Maria 80
First World War 24, 32, 48
Fitzgerald, F. Scott, *The Great Gatsby* 107
Fitzgerald, Robert 18
Florina 101–2
folk poems 101
    'The Song of Dead Brother' 101
Forster, E. M. 112, 116
    Pharos and Pharillon 116
Fowler, Rowena 117n
Frangopoulos, Th. D. 114
Friar, Kimon, 'The Use of Classical Myth
    by Modern Greek Poets' 74
Futurism 118

Gallipoli 36, 51–2, 53
Gatsos, Nikos, *Amorgos* 74, 91
Gay, John, 'Mr Pope's Welcome from
    Greece' 130, 135
Georganta, Konstantina 86–7, 112, 135
Germany 106
    Nazi regime 73
Gilmour, Ian, *The Making of the Poets:
    Byron and Shelley in Their Time* 96
Ginsberg, Allen 76-7
Gladstone, W. E., *Studies On Homer and
    the Homeric Age* 28
Glyniadakis, Krystalli 135
Gnosticism 75
Goethe, Johann Wolfgang von 67
    Faust 63
Goldsworthy, Vesna
    The Angel of Salonika 104
    'The Birthday Concert' 106
    Chernobyl Strawberries 105
    'Germany' 106
    Gorsky 106–7
    *Inventing Ruritania: The Imperialism
        of the Imagination* 105
    'Summer on Pelion' 103–4
    'Three Eighteen' 105, 106
Graves, Robert 18
Greece
    civil war 84

coup d'état (1967) 71, 71n, 74
Greek language 117
  status 10
Green, Peter 19, 55
The Guardian 97
Gulf War 41

H. D. (Hilda Doolittle) 31
Hadjidakis, Manos 75
Hardy, Thomas 118
Harrison, Tony, *Collected Poems* 43
Harsent, David 124
  In Secret: Versions of Yannis Ritsos 100
  Night 124
  'Three Poems after Cavafy' 124
    'Afternoon Sun' 124
    'The Art of Poetry' 124
    'At the Tobacconist's Window' 124
Hass, Robert 10–11, 132
Heaney, Seamus 46, 72, 117
  District and Circle 117
  'George Seferis in the Underworld' 118
Hector 19–22, 35
Hellenistic period 115, 125
Hellespont 48, 51
Heraclitus 60, 75
Hesiod, *Theogony* 60
Hill, Geoffrey 102
Hoeksema, Thomas 82
Hoffman, Eva 106
Hoggard, Liz 40
Holman, Michael 82
Homer 53, 60, 62, 97
  The Iliad 9, 17–22, 26, 47, 62, 65, 68, 111, 132, 133
  The Iliad: A New Translation (trans. Peter Green) 19
  The Iliad of Homer (trans. Alexander Pope) 19, 130
  The Iliad and the Odyssey of Homer (trans. Richmond Lattimore) 19
  The Iliad (trans. Robert Fagles) 19
  The Iliad (trans. Stanley Lombardo) 19
  The Iliads of Homer (trans. George Chapman) 18
  The Odyssey 10, 18, 41, 46, 61, 63, 130
Horace 45, 53

Hughes, Ted 41–9, 48, 133, 135
  fascination with theatre 62
  on translation 43–5
  use of cribs 43
  (trans.) *Alcestis* (Euripides) 42, 63
  Birthday Letters 42
  'Everyman's Odyssey' 41
  Landmarks and Voyages 41
  Lupercal 41
  Moortown Diary 62
  (trans.) *Oedipus* (Seneca) 41
  (trans.) *The Oresteia* (Aeschylus) 42
  Selected Translations (ed. Weissbort) 41, 43
  Tales from Ovid 42
hybridity 24, 33, 46, 50, 53, 55, 65, 92
Hypatia Trust 110

Ibycus 60, 61
Iliopoulou, Katerina 135
imitations 23–4
in-betweenness 100–111
The Independent 89
Independent on Sunday 120
influence 15–16, 24, 129, 135
  theory of 82–3
The International Literary Quarterly 134
intertextuality 32, 55, 83, 92, 133
Israel–Palestine conflict 26
Istanbul 125
Italy 73
Ithaca (Ithaka) 9, 47
Ivask, Ivar 12

James, William 87
Jeffreys, Peter, (ed.) *The Forster-Cavafy Letters: Friends at a Slight Angle* 116
Jenkins, Alan 110
Jews, Jewish tradition 72, 73
Johnson, Samuel 22, 82
Jones, Evan 111, 123
  (trans.) 'Anna Komnene' (Cavafy) 119
  (trans.) 'Apollonius of Tyana on Rhodes' (Cavafy) 119
  'Bundesland Bavaria, between Deffingen and Denzingen' 102
  'Cavafy in Liverpool' 118, 119, 129
  (ed.) *The Cavafy Reader* 119

'Constantine and Arete: an auto-
  biography' 101–2
'The Devoted Widow' 119
(trans.) 'Hidden' (Cavafy) 119
'How I Became one of my Poems' 102
(trans.) 'In the Port' (Cavafy) 119
'Journey' 102
'Justinian's Advisors Recall Him
  Prophesying' 103, 119
'Later Emperors' 119
'Letter to Sofia' 102
'Little Notes on Painting' 103
'Mr. Eugenides, the Smyrna
  Merchant' 119
Nothing Fell Today but Rain 103
(trans.) 'On Italian Shores' (Cavafy)
  119
Paralogues 101–2, 103, 119
'Santorini' 101
'Three Actaeons' 103
Joyce, James
  Finnegans Wake 23
  Ulysses 18
Jung, C. G., *Septem Sermones ad Mortuos*
  75
Juvenal 49

Kallman, Chester 43
Kampanellis, Iakovos, *Mauthausen* 73
Kantakouzenos, John 126
Kapsalis, Dionysis, 134
Karyotakis, Kostas 111
katharevousa 117
Kavounas, Alice 107, 124
  *Abandoned Gardens: Selected and
    New Poems 1995–2016* 107
  'Aivali' 107
  'Cutchogue, Long Island' 109
  'Foreign Mirrors' 108
  The Invited 107
  'Lunch in Ayvalik Harbour, Anatolia'
    109
  '*Maen Eglos*, Lizard Peninsula' 107
  'Ocean' 108
  'On Seeing the Statue of Liberty for
    the Second Time' 107
  Ornament of Asia 107
  'The Road to Ithaca' 107

'Swallowing the Sea' 108
Words in Air 109, 110
Kavvadias, Nikos 92–3
Keats, John 109, 110, 115
  'Ode on a Grecian Urn' 10
Keeley, Edmund, and Sherrard, Phillip 123
  Four Greek Poets 15
  Introduction to Elytis, *Selected Poems*
    12
Kondos, Yannis 11, 92
Kragujevac, massacre of Serbs 73
Kruczkowska, Joanna 117n, 135

Laforgue, Jules 83
Lagios, Ilias 79–80, 82, 86–7, 134
  Desolate Land 86
Latin language, status of 10
Lattimore, Richmond 19
Lessing, Doris 27
Letsios, Vassilis 83n
Levi, Peter
  Goodbye to the Art of Poetry 132–3
  The Hill of Kronos 91
Leviston, Frances 97
Lewis, Wyndham 24
Li Po 45
life-writing 32
Liverpool 115
'Living Classics' (conference, Oxford, 2005)
  57
Livy 60
Logue, Christopher 17–25, 40, 41, 47, 69,
  70, 122, 130, 133
  as constant reviser 37–8
  death 36, 39
  in prison 26, 28
  'Loyal to the King' 26
  Prince Charming 18, 25
  Selected Poems 17n, 26
  'The Song of the Dead Soldier' 26
  'The Song of the Imperial Carrion' 26
  'To My Fellow Artists' 27
  War Music 17n, 18, 22, 23, 24, 26–7,
    28, 30, 46, 48, 63, 133
    'An Account' 26, 40
    drafts and fragments 36–40
  All Day Permanent Red 17n, 24,
    35, 39

    Big Men Falling a Long Way
      17n, 37, 38
    Cold Calls 17n, 37
    GBH 17n, 35
    Kings 28, 32
    Patrocleia 10, 17n, 24, 35
    Pax 17n
Lombardo, Stanley 19
London 107, 110, 115
    anti-war movement 17
London Literature Festival 66
The London Magazine 71n
Lorca, Federico García 62
Lowell, Robert 18, 109
Lucas, John
    'The Cemetery at Molivos' 93
    'Faith and Reason: An Aeginetan Dialogue' 93
    (ed.) *The Isles of Greece: A Collection of the Poetry of Place* 92–4, 100, 109, 130
    'One for Zeno' 93
    'A Postcard from Andros' 93
Lucian 59–60
Luther, Martin 106
Lydgate, John 18

McAuliffe, John 118
MacKay, Marina 24
McKinsey, Martin, (ed.) *Clearing the Ground: Poetry and Prose, 1902–1911* 115
Mahon, Derek 117n
Maisonneuve 102n
Malanos, Timos 114–5
Malli, Morphia 82
Manguel, Alberto 87
Mansfield, Peter 73
Marathon, battle of 58
Marazion 60
Marinetti, Marino, Futurist Manifesto 24
'Martian School' 45
Massalia (later Marseille) 9
Mavrogordato, John 112, 113, 129
Menander 93
Menard, Pierre 84–5, 87
Mendelsohn, Daniel, (trans.) *The Collected Poems of C.P. Cavafy* 115

Mexico 91
Middleton, Christopher 124–5
    Collected Later Poems 124
    'Postcard from Alexandria' 125
    'The Strategy of Apanea' 125
    'The Typesetter's Visit to Cavafy' 125
    'What Could You Have Made of It, Kavafis?' 124
    'What the Hedgehog Said, A.D. 360' 124
militaria 31
Miller, George 124
Milton, John 92
    'Lycidas' 10
    Paradise Regained 18
Modern Poetry in Translation 43–5, 48, 51, 63
modernism 9–10, 22–5, 31, 39, 56, 70, 78, 83–4, 93, 133–4
Moore, Kim, *The Art of Falling* 129
Morgan, Kathleen, *Ovid's Art of Imitation: Propertius in the Amores* 53
multilingualism 83, 133–4
mythology, classical 12

New Statesman 64, 68
New York 41, 107, 109, 125
    Harlem 32
Ní Dhomhnaill, Nuala 134
Nike of Samothrace 75
Nobel Prize for Literature 12
Norfolk 110
Norris, Margot, *Writing War in the Twentieth Century* 24–5
Northcott Theatre, Exeter 42
Northern Broadsides company 42
Northern Ireland 41
nyckelharpa 66

Odysseus 9, 47, 50, 61, 132
orality 132
Orpheus 60, 75
Oswald, Alice 24, 35, 48, 133
    Dart 67–8
    Falling Awake 62, 67
    Hughes Memorial Lecture (2005) 62
    Memorial: An Excavation of the Iliad 62–70, 63, 67, 133, 135

'Severed Head Floating Downriver' 67
'Tithonus' 62, 66–7
'The Unbearable Brightness of Speaking' 65–6, 68
Outram, Richard, 'Benedict Abroad' 102
Ovid 42, 51–6, 60
   Tristia 51–7, 55–6, 57
Owen, Wilfred 35
Oxford, University of 132
Palamas, Kostis 12
Palatine Anthology 115
Palestine 26
Papageorgiou, Fani
   Not So Ill with You and Me 110–11
   'Seagulls' 111
   'The Delta' 111
   The Purloined Letter 110–11
   'Travels Without You' 111
paratexts 16, 52n, 56, 112
Paris 17, 27
Parthia 125
Paterson, Don 46
   (trans.) 'The Bowl-Maker' (Cavafy) 123
   'Fourteen Notes on the Version' 30
   Landing Light 123
   Rain 123
   'Three Poems after Cavafy' 123
      'The Bandaged Shoulder' 123
      'The Boat' 123
      'One Night' 123
Patroclus 19–22, 35, 59, 122
Pavlopoulos, George 91
Paz, Octavio 91
Pelion 75, 79, 103–4
Peloponnese 95, 99, 100
Péret, Benjamin 118
periplous 130–35
Perse, Saint-John 76, 124
Piraeus 92
Plato 60, 92
   The Republic 50
   Symposium 60
Pliny the Elder 9
Plomer, William 130
   The Fivefold Screen 112

'Sonnet to Cavafy: To the Greek Poet C. P. Cavafy on his Ποιήματα (1908–1914)' 112, 130
Plutarch 117
PN Review 119
Podularity (website) 124
Poe, Edgar Allan 83–4
Poetry Ireland Review 119
'Poetry and Melancholia' (conference) 123
poetry of place 93, 100, 109
poetry-as-cinema 33
Poland 106
Pollard, Clare 44n
Polybius 9
Pope, Alexander 17, 19, 22, 31, 130, 135
Popski's Private Army 26
Porter, Peter 89
(post)modernism 53
Pound, Ezra 31, 43, 48, 70, 89
   radio broadcasts 25
   The Cantos 11, 18, 23, 36, 132
   Cathay 22, 133
   Homage to Sextus Propertius 22, 23, 24
   'The Return' 31
   'The Seafarer' 133
Preveza 111
Propertius 49, 53
prose elements in poetry 103
Purcell, Sally 74
Pushkin, Alexander 44
Pytheas 97–8, 130–2, 135
   On the Ocean 9, 130

Rabassa, Gregory 81
Raine, Craig 45
Rakopoulos, Thodoris 135
Rayor, Diane J. 49
rebetika 75
recomposing 29
Reid, Christopher 28, 37–8, 39, 48, 130
   (trans.) 'The Circumstances' (Cavafy, 'Before Time Could Change Them') 123
   'The Cochineal' 123
   The Curiosities 123
   For and After 45, 46, 122
   Katerina Brac 45

Reynolds, Matthew 29
Ricks, David
   'Cavafy's Stationery' 116–7, 129
   The Shade of Homer: A Study in
      Modern Greek Poetry 11
Riley, Peter 111
   'Argolid 2003' 95
   'Argolid 2004' 95
   'Corcoran and Greece' 94
   'ExoMáni 2002 (10 Preludes)' 94
   'ExoMáni 2005 (10 Postludes)' 95
   Greek Passages 94
Rilke, Rainer Maria, *Duino Elegies* 104
Ritsos, Yannis 75, 99, 100, 103n
Rome 125
Romiosyne 72, 75
Rommel, Field Marshal Erwin 31, 34
Rose, Marilyn Gaddis 81
Royal Exchange Theatre, London 47
Royal Gloucester Hussars 51
Russell, Bertrand 26
Rutland 60

Sachtouris, Miltos 102, 103n
Sackler Library, Oxford 58
Samarakis, Antonis, Το Λάθος (*The Flaw*) 73
Sanderson, Griselda 66
Sappho 57, 92, 98, 131
Sarajevo, siege of 41
Saunders, Lesley 10
   Periplous: The Twelve Voyages of
      Pytheas 130–32, 133
Schechner, Richard, *Dionysus* 41
Schrott, Raoul, 'Actaeon' 103
sea voyages, imagery of 130–2
The Seafarer 132
The Second Rebel Movement 85
Second World War 17, 24, 26
Seferis, George 12, 74, 76, 82, 91, 103n, 124, 134
   'Epi Aspalathon' ('On Gorse') 92
   Mythistorema 86–7, 97
   On the Greek Style 114
   'Ο Γυρισμός του Ξενιτεμένου' ('The Return of the Exile') 109
   Ημερολόγιο Καταστρώματος, γ´ (*Logbook III*), 91
   Κίχλη ('The Thrush') 78, 79

Seneca, *Oedipus* 41
Serbia, Serbs 73, 104
Serbo-Croatian language 74
Serefas, Sakis 104n
Shakespeare, William 115
shamanism 63
Shelley, Percy Bysshe 115
   Homeric Hymns 18
Shoestring Press 92
Shuttle, Penelope 110
Sikelianos, Angelos 12
Sinfield, Alan, *Literature, Politics and Culture in Postwar Britain* 27
Sinopoulos, Takis 74
Sir Gawain and the Green Knight 47, 133
Skopje 32
Smyrna 107
Solomos, Dionysios 12, 82, 83
   'The Destruction of Psara' 85
Sophocles 42, 49, 62
   Antigone 27–8, 41
Southbank Centre, London 66
Spain 59
Spanish language 74
Spenser, Edmund 19
Stangos, Nikos 74
Stefanidis, Manos 88n
Steiner, George 9, 19, 30, 40, 45
   'Homer in English' 18
   (ed.) *Poem into Poem* 18, 22, 46
Stevens, Wallace, 'Flyer's Fall' 77
Stirling, University of 123
Stopa-Hunt, Chloe 62–3
Suetonius 117
Suffolk 110
Syria 59, 119
Szirtes, George 110

Tatum, James, *The Mourner's Song* 35
Tennyson, Alfred Lord 115
   'The Charge of the Heavy Brigade at Balaclava' 31
textual impermanence 65
Thebes 71
Theodorakis, Mikis 75
Theoharis, Theoharis C., *Before Time Could Change Them: The Collected Poems of Constantine P. Cavafy* 115

Thessaloniki (Salonika) 104, 104n
Thucydides 60, 111
Thwaite, Anthony 41, 89
Tomis 53
Tomlinson, Charles 27, 49
   Poetry and Metamorphosis 45
Topali, Maria 135
transgressions 49–50, 120
translation
   as adventure 134
   and biblical exegesis 82
   creative 22, 49–50
   and culture 30
   curated 48
   fidelity in 57
   quality of 15, 18, 26
   subjectivity in 23
   translators' statements 56
translingualism 133
Trojan War 32, 34, 48
Trypanis, C. A., *Medieval and Modern Greek Poetry* 15
Tsvetayeva, Marina 45
Turkey 111
Twickenham 130
Twombly, Cy, 'Death of Actaeon' 103
Tynan, Kenneth 27, 37
Tziovas, Dimitris 13

Ultima Thule (later Iceland) 9
Underwood, Simon 22, 23
United Kingdom 26, 104, 107, 109–10, 118–20, 135
United States of America 73, 107

Valassopoulo, George 115, 116
Valéry, Paul 45, 83
Van Dyck, Karen
   Austerity Measures: The New Greek Poetry 13
   Kassandra and the Censors: Greek Poetry Since 1967 11
Varoufakis, Yanis 14
Vassar College 107
Vayenas, Nasos 74, 76–90, 82, 84, 134
   'Clean Curtains' 114
   'The Grammarian's Melancholy' 114

The Perfect Order: Selected Poems 1974–2010 (ed. Berengarten and Nikolaou) 84
'T. S. Eliot' 84
'Η Αίθουσα' 82
Βιογραφία (*Biography*) 76
Ποίηση και Μετάφραση ('Poetry and Translation') 82
'Πάτροκλος Γιατράς, ή Οι Ελληνικές Μεταφράσεις της Έρημης Χώρας' ('Patroclus Yiatras, or, the Greek Translations of *The Waste Land*') 84–5
Η Πτώση του Ιπτάμενου ('Flyer's Fall') 77, 82
Η Πτώση του Ιπτάμενου, β´ ('Flyer's Fall II') 87–8
Σκοτεινές Μπαλλάντες και Άλλα Ποιήματα 88–9
Στη Νήσο των Μακάρων 84
Συνομιλώντας με τον Καβάφη ('Conversing with Cavafy') 113
Venuti, Lawrence 23
Verlaine, Paul 83
verset (verse-paragraph) 76, 103
Vietnam 84
Virgil 53
   Aeneid 60, 132
   Georgics 61
Vlavianos, Haris 134

Wakefield, Xanthe 17, 28
Walcott, Derek, *Omeros* 18
war, emotions about 34, 36
Weinberger, Eliot, *A Tale of Two Gardens* 91
Weissbort, Daniel 41, 43, 43–4, 45, 48
Whitbread Prize for Poetry 17
White Review 69
Whitman, Walt 76–7
Woolf, Virginia 97
Wordsworth, William 109, 110
World Literature Today 12

Xylouris, Nikos 97

Yao, Steven G., *Translation and the Languages of Modernism* 23

Yiatras, Patroclus 84–5
Yorkshire 42
Yugoslavia (former) 73, 104

Zeytinlik 104

www.ingramcontent.com/pod-product-compliance
Lightning Source LLC
Chambersburg PA
CBHW031148160426
43193CB00008B/297